LES LIAISONS DANGEREUSES

LES LIAISONS DANGEREUSES

a play by
CHRISTOPHER HAMPTON

FROM THE NOVEL BY
CHODERLOS DE LACLOS

faber and faber
LONDON · BOSTON

First published in 1985
by Faber and Faber Limited
3 Queen Square London WC1N 3AU
Revised reprint published in 1986

Photoset by Wilmaset Birkenhead Merseyside
Printed in Great Britain by
Cox & Wyman Ltd, Reading, Berkshire

A CIP record for this book is available from the British Library

ISBN 0-571-13724-5

8 10 9 7

Comme devant tant d'oeuvres de notre temps – pas seulement littéraires – le lecteur des *Liaisons* eût pu dire: 'Ça ne peut pas durer ainsi.'

André Malraux, 1969

To Roger

Les Liaisons Dangereuses opened at The Other Place,
Stratford-upon-Avon, on 24 September 1985. The cast was as
follows:

LA MARQUISE DE MERTEUIL	Lindsay Duncan
MME DE VOLANGES	Fiona Shaw
CÉCILE VOLANGES	Lesley Manville
LE VICOMTE DE VALMONT	Alan Rickman
AZOLAN	Christopher Wright
MME DE ROSEMONDE	Margery Mason
LA PRÉSIDENTE DE TOURVEL	Juliet Stevenson
ÉMILIE	Mary Jo Randle
LE CHEVALIER DANCENY	Sean Baker

Various SERVANTS in the Merteuil, Rosemonde, Tourvel
and Valmont households

Director Howard Davies
Designer Bob Crowley

The action takes place in various salons and bedrooms in a
number of hôtels and châteaux in and around Paris, and in the
Bois de Vincennes, one autumn and winter in the 1780s.

AUTHOR'S NOTE

What is published here is the text of the play as it stood on the
first day of rehearsal; and the various minor cuts and abrasions
(and improvements) sustained and effected during rehearsals are
therefore not included

A NOTE ON LACLOS

In many respects, Pierre-Ambroise-François Choderlos de Laclos (1741–1803) is the perfect author: he wrote, at around the age of forty, one piece of fiction, which was not merely a masterpiece, but the supreme example of its genre, the epistolary novel; and then troubled the public no further.

Fortunately the obscurity from which, during his lifetime, this astonishing *tour de force* delivered him only briefly, has remained sufficiently deep to preserve his enigma. But those few facts which are known about him combine to throw an intriguing light on his vigorously classical novel.

A career soldier in an unusually extended period of peace, Laclos volunteered to serve in the American War of Independence, but lacked the means necessary to a campaign officer at the time. Instead, he was posted to a drab island in the Bay of Biscay and put in charge of its fortification. It was from here, bored and disappointed, that he wrote, famously, to a friend, announcing his intention to write something 'out of the ordinary, eyecatching, something that would resound around the world even after I had left it'. Few artists can have fulfilled their predictions so satisfactorily.

The novel caused an immediate and continuing sensation, and in its wake Laclos addressed himself to two other pieces of work: a treatise on women's education, unpublished in his lifetime; and a blistering demolition of one of France's military sacred cows, the tactician Maréchal de Vauban, which caused such offence that he was immediately rewarded with a series of particularly dreary provincial postings.

In the Revolution he was a Jacobin, not prominent but assiduous, a friend of Danton and the associate and secretary of the Duc d'Orléans, the king's liberal cousin, known as Philippe-Égalité. Inevitably during the Terror he was jailed twice and escaped execution, which he clearly expected, only narrowly and for reasons which have remained obscure. It took some time for him to be accepted back into the army, but eventually at the turn of the century he was made a general by Napoleon. The result, however, of this final success, was that only a few weeks after arriving in Taranto in Southern Italy to take up a new command, he died of dysentery and malaria. His last letter was a dignified but urgent appeal to Napoleon, asking for support for his wife and three children.

Geometrician, inventor, military strategist, feminist, revolutionary, devoted husband and father: all of these qualities, some initially surprising in the author of *Les Liaisons Dangereuses*, others less so, make their contribution towards a way of looking at this extraordinary and meteoric work: without, however, exhausting the pleasures of its rare mystery and merciless intelligence.

Christopher Hampton

ACT I

ONE

A warm evening in August. The principal salon in the Paris hôtel of Mme la Marquise de Merteuil. The MARQUISE, *a respectable widow of considerable means, is playing piquet with her cousin,* MME DE VOLANGES, *who is herself a widow. Sitting next to* MME DE VOLANGES, *watching her play and politely stifling the occasional yawn, is her daughter* CÉCILE, *a slim and attractive blonde girl of 15. Suggestions of great opulence. The large playing cards slap down on one another.* MERTEUIL *interrupts the game to examine* CÉCILE *with some care.*

MERTEUIL: Well, my dear.
（CÉCILE, *who has been daydreaming, starts, not quite sure, for a second, if it's she who's being addressed.*）
So you've left the convent for good?

CÉCILE: Yes, Madame.

MERTEUIL: And how are you adapting to the outside world?

CÉCILE: Very well, I think. I'm so excited to have my own bedroom and dressing room.

VOLANGES: I've advised her to watch and learn and be quiet except when spoken to. She's very naturally still prone to confusion. Yesterday she was under the impression my shoemaker had come for dinner.

CÉCILE: It wasn't that, Maman, it was when he fell to his knees and caught hold of my foot. It startled me.

MERTEUIL: No doubt you thought he was attempting to propose marriage.

CÉCILE: I . . .
（*She breaks off, blushing.*）

MERTEUIL: Never mind, my dear, you'll soon get used to it. We must see what we can devise for your amusement.
（*The game resumes. Silence. After a time, Merteuil's* MAJORDOMO *appears, advances unhurriedly across the room and murmurs something in* MERTEUIL's *ear.* MERTEUIL *sighs.*）

9

Oh, very well, show him up.

(*The* MAJORDOMO *bows and withdraws.* MERTEUIL *turns back to the others.*)

Valmont is here.

VOLANGES: You receive him, do you?

MERTEUIL: Yes. So do you.

VOLANGES: I thought perhaps that under the circumstances . . .

MERTEUIL: Under what circumstances? I don't believe I have any grounds for self-reproach . . .

VOLANGES: On the contrary. As far as I know, you're virtually unique in that respect.

MERTEUIL: . . . and, of course, if I had, he would no longer be calling on me.

(CÉCILE *has been following this exchange closely, frowning in the attempt to make sense of it. Now* MME DE VOLANGES *turns to her.*)

VOLANGES: Monsieur le Vicomte de Valmont, my child, whom you very probably don't remember, except that he is conspicuously charming, never opens his mouth without first calculating what damage he can do.

CÉCILE: Then why do you receive him, Maman?

VOLANGES: Everyone receives him. He has a distinguished name, a large fortune and a very pleasant manner. You'll soon find that society is riddled with such inconsistencies: we're all aware of them, we all deplore them and in the end we all accommodate to them. Besides which, people are quite rightly afraid to provoke his malice. No one has the slightest respect for him; but everyone is very nice to him.

(*She breaks off as the* MAJORDOMO *reappears, escorting* LE VICOMTE DE VALMONT, *a strikingly elegant figure.* VALMONT *crosses the room and bows formally to* MERTEUIL *in a gesture which also takes in the others.*)

VALMONT: Madame.

MERTEUIL: Vicomte.

VOLANGES: What a pleasant surprise.

VALMONT: How delightful to see you, Madame.

VOLANGES: You remember my daughter, Cécile.

VALMONT: Well, indeed, but who could have foretold she

would flower so gracefully?

(CÉCILE *simpers and looks away.* VALMONT *turns back to* MERTEUIL.)

I wanted to call on you before leaving the city.

MERTEUIL: Oh, I'm not sure we can allow that. Why should you want to leave?

VALMONT: Paris in August, you know: and it's time I paid a visit on my old aunt, I've neglected her disgracefully.

MERTEUIL: I approve of your aunt. She takes such an intelligent interest in the young, she's been able to maintain a kind of youthfulness of her own. All the same . . .

VOLANGES: Will you please give Madame de Rosemonde our warmest regards? She's been good enough to invite us to stay at the château, and I hope perhaps later in the season . . .

VALMONT: I shall make a point of it, Madame. Please don't let me interrupt your game.

VOLANGES: I think I may have lost enough for this evening.

(*In the ensuing silence, they become aware that* CÉCILE *is fast asleep.*)

VALMONT: Your daughter evidently finds our conversation intriguing.

(*He laughs and* MERTEUIL *joins in, causing* CÉCILE *to jerk awake in confusion.*)

CÉCILE: Oh, I'm sorry, I . . .

VOLANGES: I think it's time we took you home.

CÉCILE: I'm used to being asleep by nine at the convent.

VALMONT: So I should hope.

(*The ladies have risen to their feet by now and* MERTEUIL *signals to a* FOOTMAN, *who moves over to escort* MME DE VOLANGES *and* CÉCILE *from the room, amid general salutations.* VALMONT *has bowed to them and now waits, a little apart. Eventually,* MERTEUIL *moves back towards him. They're alone together and look at each other for a while before* MERTEUIL *speaks, in a quite different tone.*)

MERTEUIL: Your aunt?

VALMONT: That's right.

MERTEUIL: Whatever for? I thought she'd already made

arrangements to leave you all her money.

VALMONT: She has. But there are other considerations, family obligations, that kind of thing.

MERTEUIL: Do you know why I summoned you here this evening?

VALMONT: I'd hoped it might be for the pleasure of my company.

MERTEUIL: I need you; to carry out a heroic enterprise. Something for your memoirs.

VALMONT: I don't know when I shall ever find the time to write my memoirs.

MERTEUIL: Then I'll write them.

(*Silence.* VALMONT *smiles at her.*)

You remember when Gercourt left me?

VALMONT: Yes.

MERTEUIL: And went off with that fat mistress of yours, whose name escapes me?

VALMONT: Yes, yes.

MERTEUIL: No one has ever done that to me before. Or to you, I imagine.

VALMONT: I was quite relieved to be rid of her, frankly.

MERTEUIL: No, you weren't.

(*Silence.*)

One of Gercourt's more crass and boring topics of conversation was what exactly he would look for in a wife, what qualities, when the moment came for him, as he put it, to settle down.

VALMONT: Yes.

MERTEUIL: He had a ludicrous theory that blondes were inherently more modest and respectable than any other species of girl and he was also unshakeably prejudiced in favour of convent education. And now he's found the ideal candidate.

VALMONT: Cécile Volanges?

MERTEUIL: Very good.

VALMONT: And her sixty thousand a year, that must have played some part in his calculations.

MERTEUIL: I tell you, if she were an uncloistered brunette, she could be worth twice that, and he wouldn't go near her. His priority, you see, is a guaranteed virtue.

VALMONT: I wonder if I'm beginning to guess what it is you're intending to propose.

MERTEUIL: Gercourt is with his regiment in Corsica until October. That should give you plenty of time.

VALMONT: You mean to . . . ?

MERTEUIL: She's a rosebud.

VALMONT: You think so?

MERTEUIL: And he'd get back from honeymoon to find himself the laughing-stock of Paris.

VALMONT: Well . . .

MERTEUIL: Yes. Love and revenge: two of your favourites. (*Silence.* VALMONT *considers for a moment. Finally, he shakes his head, smiling.*)

VALMONT: No, I can't.

MERTEUIL: What?

VALMONT: You know how difficult I find it to disobey your orders. But really, I can't.

MERTEUIL: Why not?

VALMONT: It's too easy. It is. What is she, 15, she's seen nothing, she knows nothing, she's bound to be curious, she'd be on her back before you'd unwrapped the first bunch of flowers. Any one of a dozen men could manage it. I have my reputation to think of.

MERTEUIL: I think you underestimate her. She's very pretty, and she has a rather promising air of languor.

VALMONT: You mean, she falls asleep a lot? Well, perhaps your Belleroche is the man for her.

MERTEUIL: Belleroche is an idealist.

VALMONT: Oh, bad luck, I knew there was something the matter with him.

MERTEUIL: There is someone who's already fallen for her: young Danceny. He goes round to sing duets with her.

VALMONT: And you think he'd like to try a little close harmony?

MERTEUIL: Yes, but he's as timid and inexperienced as she is, we couldn't rely on him. So, you see, it'll just have to be you.

VALMONT: I hate to disappoint you.

MERTEUIL: I think you really are going to refuse me. Aren't you?

(*Silence.* VALMONT *looks at her.*)

VALMONT: I can see I'm going to have to tell you everything.

MERTEUIL: Of course you are.

VALMONT: Yes. Well. My trip to the country to visit my more or less immortal aunt. The fact of the matter is that it's the first step towards the most ambitious plan I've ever undertaken.

MERTEUIL: Well, go on.

VALMONT: You see, my aunt is not on her own just at the moment. She has a young friend staying with her. Madame de Tourvel.

MERTEUIL: Yes.

VALMONT: She is my plan.

MERTEUIL: You can't mean it.

VALMONT: Why not? To seduce a woman famous for strict morals, religious fervour and the happiness of her marriage: what could possibly be more prestigious?

MERTEUIL: I think there's something very degrading about having a husband for a rival. It's humiliating if you fail and commonplace if you succeed. Where is he, anyway?

VALMONT: He's presiding over some labyrinthine case in Burgundy, which I'm reliably informed will drag on for months.

MERTEUIL: I can't believe this. Apart from anything else, she's such a frump. Bodice up to her ears in case you might catch a glimpse of a square inch of flesh . . .

VALMONT: You're right, clothes don't suit her.

MERTEUIL: How old is she?

VALMONT: Twenty-two.

MERTEUIL: And she's been married . . . ?

VALMONT: Two years.

MERTEUIL: Even if you succeed, you know what?

VALMONT: What?

MERTEUIL: All you'll get from her is what she gives her husband. I don't think you can hope for any actual

14

pleasure. They never let themselves go, those people. If you ever make her heart beat faster, it won't be love, it'll be fear. I sometimes wonder about you, Vicomte. How could you make such a fool of yourself over a complete nonentity?

VALMONT: Take care, now, you're speaking of the woman I . . .

MERTEUIL: Yes?

VALMONT: I've set my heart on.

(*Silence. He smiles at her.*)

I haven't felt so strongly about anything since you and I were together.

MERTEUIL: And you're going to pass up this wonderful opportunity for revenge?

VALMONT: If I have to.

MERTEUIL: You don't have to. I won't tell anyone about this bizarre aberration of yours.

VALMONT: I think you'll have to wait at least until I've had her before I can allow you to insult her. And I can't agree with your theory about pleasure. You see, I have no intention of breaking down her prejudices. I want her to believe in God and virtue and the sanctity of marriage, and still not be able to stop herself. I want passion, in other words. Not the kind we're used to, which is as cold as it's superficial, I don't get much pleasure out of that any more. No. I want the excitement of watching her betray everything that's most important to her. Surely you understand that. I thought betrayal was your favourite word.

MERTEUIL: No, no, cruelty, I always think that has a nobler ring to it.

VALMONT: You're terrible, you're a hundred times worse than I'll ever be; since we started this little mission, you've made many more converts than I have, you make me feel like an amateur.

MERTEUIL: And so you are; really, you might just as well be in love.

VALMONT: Well, if love is not being able to think of anything else all day or dream of anyone else all night, perhaps I am:

15

that's why I must have her, to rescue myself from this ridiculous position.

MERTEUIL: Love is something you use, not something you fall into, like a quicksand, don't you remember? It's like medicine, you use it as a lubricant to nature.

(*They look at each other.*)

VALMONT: How is Belleroche?

MERTEUIL: Well, he *is* in love. I thought it might be time to end it last week, I tried to pick a quarrel, but he looked so woebegone, I relented, and we spent the best night we've ever had. Since then, of course, he's been more assiduous than ever. But I'm keeping him at arm's length because I'm so pleased with him. He hasn't learned that excess is something you reserve for people you're about to leave.

VALMONT: So you're not about to leave him?

MERTEUIL: No, I told you, at the moment I'm very pleased with him.

VALMONT: And he's currently your only lover?

MERTEUIL: Yes.

VALMONT: I think you should take another. I think it most unhealthy, this exclusivity.

MERTEUIL: You're not jealous, are you?

VALMONT: Well, of course I am. Belleroche is completely undeserving.

MERTEUIL: I thought he was one of your closest friends.

VALMONT: Exactly, so I know what I'm talking about. No, I think you should organize an infidelity. With me, for example.

MERTEUIL: But we decided it was far more important to preserve our friendship and to be able to trust each other implicitly.

VALMONT: Are you sure that wasn't just a device to heighten our pleasure?

MERTEUIL: You refuse to grant me a simple favour, and then you expect to be indulged.

VALMONT: It's only because it is so simple. It wouldn't feel like a conquest. I have to follow my destiny, you see. I have to be true to my profession.

MERTEUIL: Well . . .

(*Long silence. They look at each other,* MERTEUIL *amused,* VALMONT *eager.*)

In that case, come back when you've succeeded with Madame de Tourvel.

VALMONT: Yes?

MERTEUIL: And I will offer you . . . a reward.

VALMONT: My love.

MERTEUIL: But I shall require proof.

VALMONT: Certainly.

MERTEUIL: Written proof.

VALMONT: Ah.

MERTEUIL: Not negotiable.

(VALMONT *rises to his feet and bows.* MERTEUIL *watches him, smiling.*)

VALMONT: And I'm sure you'll find someone to help you out with the little Volanges.

MERTEUIL: She's so lovely. If my morals were less austere, I'd take it on myself.

VALMONT: You are an astonishing woman.

MERTEUIL: Thank you.

VALMONT: I'm only sorry you haven't sufficient confidence in me to give me my reward in advance.

MERTEUIL: Goodnight, Vicomte.

(*He kisses her hand, releases it and stands looking at her for a moment, before turning away.*)

TWO

Three weeks later. Early evening. The principal salon in Mme de Rosemonde's château in the country. The late sun slants through the french windows. VALMONT *is interviewing* AZOLAN, *his* valet de chambre, *a dapper young man, resplendent in the livery of a* chasseur.

VALMONT: So he grasped what was going on, did he?

AZOLAN: Oh, yes, sir. I was watching him and he was watching you.

VALMONT: I just hope he was better at understanding what was happening than he was at shadowing me; I sat down for a rest on the way and he was trampling about behind some bush, making so much noise I had a good mind to give him a legful of small shot. Except then I suppose he'd have had even more trouble keeping up.

AZOLAN: He knew what you were doing: and after you'd gone he talked to the family.

VALMONT: I must say the family was very well chosen.

AZOLAN: Thank you, sir.

VALMONT: Solidly respectable, gratifyingly tearful, no suspiciously pretty girls. Well done.

AZOLAN: I do my best for you, sir.

VALMONT: And not even unduly expensive. Fifty-six livres to save an entire family from ruin, that seems a genuine bargain.

AZOLAN: These days, my lord, you can find half a dozen like that, any village in the country.

VALMONT: Really? I must say, it's no longer a mystery to me why people fall so easily into the habit of charitable enterprises. All that humble gratitude. It was most affecting.

AZOLAN: Certainly brought a tear to my eye, sir.

VALMONT: How are you getting on with the maid?

AZOLAN: Julie? Tell you the truth, it's been a bit boring. If I

wasn't so anxious to keep your lordship abreast, I think I'd
only have bothered the once. I'm not sure she doesn't feel
the same, but, you know, what else is there to do in the
country?

VALMONT: Yes, it wasn't so much the details of your intimacy I
was after, it was whether she's agreed to bring me Madame
de Tourvel's letters and do you think she'll keep her mouth
shut?

AZOLAN: She won't steal the letters, sir.

VALMONT: She won't?

AZOLAN: You know better than me, sir, it's easy enough
making them do what they want to do; it's trying to get
them to do what you want them to do, that's what gives you
a headache.

VALMONT: And them, as often as not.

AZOLAN: As for keeping her mouth shut, I haven't asked her to
keep her mouth shut, because that's the one thing most
likely to give her the idea of opening it.

VALMONT: You may well be right. But look, Madame de
Tourvel told me she'd been warned about me: that means
some officious friend must have written to her about me. I
need to know who.

AZOLAN: I shouldn't worry about all that, if I was you, sir. If
she's interested enough to have you followed, I'd say it was
only a matter of time.

VALMONT: Do you think so?

AZOLAN: Anyway, apparently she keeps her letters in her
pockets.

VALMONT: I wish I knew how to pick pockets. Why don't our
parents ever teach us anything useful?
(*Pause, as* VALMONT *considers.*)
Where do you and Julie meet?

AZOLAN: Oh, in my room, sir.

VALMONT: And is she coming tonight?

AZOLAN: Afraid so.

VALMONT: Then I think I may have to burst in on you. See if
blackmail will succeed better than bribery. About two
o'clock suit you? I don't want to embarrass you, will that

19

give you enough time?

AZOLAN: Ample, sir.

VALMONT: Good.

AZOLAN: Then you won't have to pay her, sir, will you?

VALMONT: Oh, I think if she delivers, we can afford to be
generous, don't you?

AZOLAN: It's your money, sir.

VALMONT: Don't worry, I shan't overlook your contribution.

AZOLAN: Well, that's very decent of you, sir.

(VALMONT *looks up at the sound of approaching female voices.
He turns back to* AZOLAN.)

VALMONT: Off you go, then. See you at two.

AZOLAN: Right, sir. I'll be sure to arrange her so she can't say
she's there to borrow a clothes brush.

(*He leaves by one door as* MME DE ROSEMONDE *and* MME
DE TOURVEL *arrive by another.* MME DE ROSEMONDE *is 84,
arthritic but lively, intelligent and sympathetic; and* MME DE
TOURVEL *is a handsome woman of 22, dressed not as Merteuil
described, but in an elegantly plain linen gown. She is clearly in
a state of considerable excitement.*)

ROSEMONDE: Here he is. I said he would be here.

(VALMONT *rises to greet them.* TOURVEL *cannot help reacting
to his presence.*)

VALMONT: Ladies.

ROSEMONDE: Madame de Tourvel has some mystery to reveal
to us.

TOURVEL: To you, Madame, to you.

VALMONT: Oh, well, then, perhaps I should go for a walk.

TOURVEL: No, no, it, it concerns you as well, I mean, it
particularly concerns you. In fact, I must begin by asking
you some questions.

VALMONT: Very well. Just let me help my aunt to her chair.

ROSEMONDE: Thank you, my boy.

(VALMONT *installs* MME DE ROSEMONDE *in her armchair,
then turns his attention back to* MME DE TOURVEL.)

VALMONT: Now.

TOURVEL: Where did you go this morning, Monsieur?

VALMONT: Well, as you know, I was up early to go out hunting.

TOURVEL: And did you succeed in making a kill this time?

VALMONT: No, I've had the most wretched luck ever since I arrived here. Also I'm a terrible shot.

TOURVEL: But on this occasion, Monsieur le Vicomte, what exactly was it you were hunting?

VALMONT: I'm sorry, I'm afraid I don't quite follow . . .

TOURVEL: You may as well own up, Monsieur, I know where you were this morning.

ROSEMONDE: I think it's time somebody explained to me what's going on.

TOURVEL: Georges, my footman, just happened to be in the village earlier today . . .

VALMONT: I do hope you haven't been listening to servants' gossip.

TOURVEL: I can see Monsieur de Valmont is determined not to tell you, so I shall have to. There's a family in the village, the man has been ill, he found himself not able to pay his taxes this year. So this morning the bailiff arrived to seize their few sticks of furniture. Whereupon your nephew, whose valet had been making enquiries in the village to see if anyone was suffering from particular hardship, arrived, paid off the family's debts and added a generous contribution to help them back on their feet again.

ROSEMONDE: Is this true, my dear?

VALMONT: Well, I . . . it's simply . . . Yes.

(MME DE ROSEMONDE *rises to her feet and spreads out her arms.*)

ROSEMONDE: You dear boy, come and let me give you a hug!

(VALMONT *crosses to her and they embrace. Then* VALMONT *turns and advances towards* MME DE TOURVEL, *smiling radiantly, his arms outstretched. A spasm of panic crosses her face but she has no choice but to submit to the embrace:* VALMONT *squeezes her powerfully. Then he releases her and, as she looks at him, ashen and mesmerized, he turns aside, wiping away a surreptitious tear.*)

It's so like you to make a secret of something like that.

(*In the ensuing silence,* MME DE TOURVEL *moves across to the tapestry frame, and picks up the already-threaded needle. But*

21

her hands are shaking so badly, she has to put it down again.)
We must visit this family in the morning, my dear, to see if
we can help in any other way.

TOURVEL: Yes, I'd like that.

VALMONT: Do sit down, aunt.

ROSEMONDE: No, I must try to find Monsieur le Curé. I shan't
be long, but I do want to tell him about this before he
leaves, he'll be so pleased.

(*She bustles out of the room, and a long silence ensues.* MME DE
TOURVEL *makes a renewed and determined effort to get to grips
with her tapestry;* VALMONT *finds a chair facing her, watches
and waits. The light is beginning to die. Finally,* MME DE
TOURVEL, *struggling for composure, feels compelled to break
the silence.*)

TOURVEL: I can't understand how someone whose instincts are
so generous could lead such a dissolute life.

VALMONT: I'm afraid you have an exaggerated idea both of my
generosity and of my depravity. If I knew who'd given you
such a dire account of me, I might be able to defend myself;
since I don't, let me make a confession: I'm afraid the key
to the paradox lies in a certain weakness of character.

TOURVEL: I don't see how so thoughtful an act of charity could
be described as weak.

VALMONT: This appalling reputation of mine, you see, there is
some justification for it. I've spent my life surrounded by
immoral people; I've allowed myself to be influenced by
them and sometimes even taken pride in outshining them.
Whereas, in this case, I've simply fallen under a quite
opposite kind of influence: yours.

TOURVEL: You mean you wouldn't have done it . . . ?

VALMONT: Not without your example, no. It was by way of an
innocent tribute to your goodness.

(*There's a pause, during which* MME DE TOURVEL, *uncertain
how to react, abandons her tapestry, hovers indecisively for a
second and then sits, perching on the edge of a chaise-longue.*)
You see how weak I am? I promised myself I was never
going to tell you. It's just, looking at you . . .

TOURVEL: Monsieur.

22

VALMONT: You needn't worry, I have no illicit intentions, I wouldn't dream of insulting you. But I do love you. I adore you.

(*He's across the room in an instant, drops to one knee in front of her and takes her hands in his.*)

Please help me!

(MME DE TOURVEL *wrenches her hands free and bursts into tears.*)

What is it?

TOURVEL: I'm so unhappy!

(*She buries her face in her hands, sobbing. For an instant, a shadow of a smile twitches across* VALMONT's *face, before he speaks in a voice on the edge of tears.*)

VALMONT: But why?

TOURVEL: Will you leave me now?

(VALMONT *rises and moves away across the room, ostensibly making an effort to control himself.*)

VALMONT: I shouldn't have said anything, I know I shouldn't, I'm sorry. But really, you have nothing to fear. Nothing at all. Tell me what to do, show me how to behave, I'll do anything you say.

(MME DE TOURVEL *manages to control herself and looks up at him.*)

TOURVEL: I thought the least I could hope for was that you would respect me.

VALMONT: But I do, of course I do!

TOURVEL: Then forget all this, don't say another word, you've offended me deeply, it's unforgivable.

VALMONT: I thought you might at least give me some credit for being honest.

TOURVEL: On the contrary, this confirms everything I've been told about you. I'm beginning to think you may well have planned the whole exercise.

VALMONT: When I came to visit my aunt, I had no idea you were here: not that it would have disturbed me in the slightest if I had known. You see, up until then, I'd only ever experienced desire. Love, never.

TOURVEL: That's enough.

VALMONT: No, no, you made an accusation, you must allow me the opportunity to defend myself. Now, you were there when my aunt asked me to stay a little longer, and at that time I only agreed in deference to her, although I was already by no means unaware of your beauty.

TOURVEL: Monsieur . . .

VALMONT: No, the point is, all this has nothing to do with your beauty. As I got to know you, I began to realize that beauty is the least of your qualities. I became fascinated by your goodness, I was drawn in by it, I didn't understand what was happening to me, and it was only when I began to feel actual physical pain every time you left the room, that it finally dawned on me: I was in love, for the first time in my life. I knew it was hopeless, of course, but that didn't matter to me, because it wasn't like it always had been, it wasn't that I wanted to have you, no. All I wanted was to deserve you.

(MME DE TOURVEL *rises decisively to her feet.*)

TOURVEL: I really will have to leave you, Monsieur, you seem determined to persist with a line of argument you must know I ought not to listen to and I don't want to hear.

VALMONT: No, no, please, sit down, sit down. I've already told you, I'll do anything you say.

(*Silence. They watch each other. Eventually,* MME DE TOURVEL *sits down again.*)

TOURVEL: There's only one thing I would like you to do for me.

VALMONT: What? What is it?

TOURVEL: But I don't see how I can ask you, I'm not even sure if I want to put myself in the position of being beholden to you.

VALMONT: Oh, please, no, I insist, if you're good enough to give me an opportunity to do something you want, anything, it's I who will be beholden to you.

(MME DE TOURVEL *looks at him for a moment with characteristic openness.*)

TOURVEL: Very well, then, I would like you to leave this house.

(*There flashes momentarily across* VALMONT's *face the expression of a chess champion who has just lost his queen.*)

24

VALMONT: I don't see why that should be necessary.

TOURVEL: Let's just say you've spent your life making it necessary.

(*By now,* VALMONT *has recovered his equilibrium; and thought very fast.*)

VALMONT: Well then, of course, whatever you say. I couldn't possibly refuse you.

(*It's* MME DE TOURVEL's *turn to be surprised.*)

Will you allow me to give my aunt, say, twenty-four hours' notice?

TOURVEL: Well, yes, naturally.

VALMONT: I shall find something in my mail tomorrow morning which obliges me to return at once to Paris.

TOURVEL: Thank you, I'd be very grateful.

VALMONT: Perhaps I might be so bold as to ask a favour in return.

(MME DE TOURVEL *frowns, hesitating.*)

I think it would only be just to let me know which of your friends has blackened my name.

TOURVEL: You know very well that's impossible, Monsieur. If friends of mine have warned me against you, they've done so purely in my own interest and I could hardly reward them with betrayal, could I? I must say, you devalue your generous offer if you want to use it as a bargaining point.

VALMONT: Very well, I withdraw the request. I hope you won't think I'm bargaining if I ask you to let me write to you.

TOURVEL: Well . . .

VALMONT: And hope that you will do me the kindness of answering my letters.

TOURVEL: I'm not sure a correspondence with you is something a woman of honour could permit herself.

VALMONT: So you're determined to refuse all my suggestions, however respectable?

TOURVEL: I didn't say that.

VALMONT: I really don't see how you could possibly be harmed by conceding me this very minor but, as far as I'm concerned, vitally important consolation.

TOURVEL: I would welcome the chance to prove to you that

what motivates me in this is not hatred or resentment,
but . . .

VALMONT: But what?

(*But* MME DE TOURVEL *seems unable to find a satisfactory
answer to this. And, moving as suddenly and swiftly as before,*
VALMONT *again crosses the room, drops to one knee and takes
her hand. She struggles to free it.*)

TOURVEL: For God's sake, Monsieur, please, leave me alone!

VALMONT: I only want to say what I hardly thought it would be
possible for me to say to you: goodbye.

(*He kisses her hand. She submits briefly, her expression
anguished, then begins to struggle again, whereupon he releases
her instantly, rises to his feet and bows.*)

I'll write soon.

(*He hurries away into the darkness, just failing to muffle a
discreet sob.* MME DE TOURVEL *is left alone, rooted to the
chaise-longue. She looks terrified.*)

THREE

A couple of days later. The middle of the night. A bedroom in a house on the outskirts of Paris which belongs to ÉMILIE, *a courtesan. She's in bed with* VALMONT, *lying in his arms, her eyes flashing in the candlelight. He seems lost in thought.* ÉMILIE *shifts her position and he smiles down at her.*

VALMONT: I thought the Dutch were supposed to be famous for their capacity for alcohol.

ÉMILIE: Three bottles of burgundy and a bottle of cognac would finish anybody.

VALMONT: Did he drink that much?

ÉMILIE: You were pouring.

VALMONT: I hope you're not missing him.

ÉMILIE: Don't be silly. I just don't think it was necessary to bundle him into your carriage.

VALMONT: Man in that condition, I thought it best to send him back to his house.

ÉMILIE: This is his house.

VALMONT: Oh. I thought it was your house.

ÉMILIE: He owns it. I just live in it. And he's so rarely in France. Seems a shame.
(*She grins broadly.*)

VALMONT: Oh, well, I'm sure my coachman will use his imagination.

ÉMILIE: I'm sure, since you're perfectly aware of the position and have no doubt given him explicit instructions, he won't have to.

VALMONT: Explicit instructions?

ÉMILIE: Yes.
(*Silence.*)

VALMONT: I must say, Émilie, I do think it's the height of bad manners to talk about some foreigner when you're in bed with me. I think some appropriate punishment is called for. Turn over.

27

(ÉMILIE *hesitates, looking up at him for a moment. Then she breaks into a smile.*)

ÉMILIE: All right.

(*She does so, looking up at him expectantly.*)

VALMONT: Now, do you have pen, ink and writing paper?

(ÉMILIE *is puzzled. After a while, she answers.*)

ÉMILIE: Yes, over there, in the bureau. Why?

(*Instead of answering,* VALMONT *gets out of bed, crosses the room, finds what he's looking for in the bureau and brings it back to the bed. He puts down the pen and inkwell carefully, twitches back the bedclothes, spreads a sheet of paper across the small of* ÉMILIE's *back, arranges himself comfortably and reaches for the pen.*)

VALMONT: Now don't move.

(ÉMILIE *is still puzzled. But she submits graciously enough.* VALMONT *begins to write.*)

'My dear Madame de Tourvel . . . I have just come . . . to my desk . . .'

(ÉMILIE *understands now. She turns her head to smile up at him.*)

Don't move, I said.

(*He resumes.*)

'. . . in the middle of a stormy night, during which I have been tossed from exaltation to exhaustion and back again. The position in which I find myself as I write has made me more than ever aware of the power of love. I can scarcely control myself sufficiently to put my thoughts in order; but despite these torments I guarantee that at this moment I am far happier than you. I hope one day you may feel the kind of disturbance afflicting me now: meanwhile please excuse me while I take steps to calm what I can only describe as a mounting excitement.'

(*He moves aside paper, pen and inkwell and leans back to nuzzle* ÉMILIE, *who hasn't moved.*)

We'll finish it later, shall we?

(*The lights fade to black.*)

FOUR

Ten days later. A September afternoon. VALMONT *is taking tea with* LA MARQUISE DE MERTEUIL *in her grand salon.*

MERTEUIL: It sounds to me as if you made a serious tactical error. Shouldn't you have taken Madame de Tourvel there and then on the chaise-longue?

VALMONT: I was expecting my aunt and the curé to appear at any moment.

MERTEUIL: Well, it would have been the most interesting thing to happen to them for years.

VALMONT: No, it wasn't at all the moment: I want her to surrender, but not before she's put up a fight.

MERTEUIL: She seems to be: she's succeeded in getting rid of you altogether.

VALMONT: But I got her to agree to let me write to her.

MERTEUIL: Well, in the unlikely event of her defences being pierced by your eloquence, you're not going to be there to take advantage of it, are you? And by the following day they'll be back in full repair.

VALMONT: Naturally, writing to someone is a poor substitute, but since I really had no choice in the matter, at least I've found a way to keep the thing alive.

MERTEUIL: Perhaps.

VALMONT: I know you're incurably sceptical, but for me, with a woman, this is by far the best stage, it's what men talk about all the time but hardly ever experience, the real intoxication: when you know she loves you, but you're still not quite certain of victory.

MERTEUIL: You know she loves you, then?

VALMONT: Oh, yes. I left my man there to keep an eye on things and a hand on the maid, who's been most co-operative since I caught them in bed together: and he tells me that when my first letter arrived, she took it to her room and sat turning it over for hours, sighing and

weeping. So it seems a reasonable enough conclusion.
(MERTEUIL *says nothing, but her expression remains dubious*.)
And the maid helped us to another discovery which might
interest you.

MERTEUIL: Oh, yes?

VALMONT: Can you guess who it was who kept writing to my
beauty, warning her to steer clear of the world's vilest
pervert, namely me? Your damned cousin, the Volanges
bitch.
(MERTEUIL *bursts out laughing*.)
It's all very well for you to laugh, she's set me back at least
a month.

MERTEUIL: It's not that.

VALMONT: She wanted me away from Madame de Tourvel: well,
now I am and I intend to make her suffer for it. Your plan to
ruin her daughter: are you making any progress? Is there
anything I can do to help? I'm entirely at your disposal.

MERTEUIL: Well, as a matter of fact, my dear Vicomte, your
presence here today forms part of my plan. I'm expecting
Danceny at any moment and I want you to help me stiffen
his resolve, if that's the phrase. And then I've arranged a
little scene I hope you may find entertaining: yes, I'm sure
you will.

VALMONT: Is that all you're going to say?

MERTEUIL: Yes, I think so.

VALMONT: Has Danceny not been a great success?

MERTEUIL: He's been disastrous. Like most intellectuals, he's
intensely stupid. He really is a most incompetent boy.
Charming, but hopeless.

VALMONT: You'd better bring me up to date.

MERTEUIL: Well, I've become extremely thick with little
Cécile. We go to my box at the Opéra and chatter away all
evening. I'm really quite jealous of whoever's in store for
her. She has a certain innate duplicity which is going to
stand her in very good stead. She has no character and no
morals, she's altogether delicious.

VALMONT: But what's happened?

MERTEUIL: She and Danceny are head over heels in love. It

started when she asked me if it would be wrong for her to write to him. First I said yes and later I said no, it would be all right, as long as she showed me both sides of the correspondence. Then I arranged a meeting, but Danceny was so paralysed with chivalry, he didn't lay a finger on her. All his energies go into writing her poems of great ingenuity and minimum impact. I tried to ginger things up by telling her it was Gercourt her mother intended her to marry. She was shocked enough to discover he was a geriatric of 36, but by the time I'd finished describing him, she couldn't have hated him more if they'd been married ten years. Then, the first major setback: she told her confessor and he took a very strong line. So she severed relations with Danceny and spent all her time praying to be able to forget him, a pleasantly self-contradictory exercise. He remained abject throughout. The only thing I could do was to organize a rendezvous for them to say goodbye to one another and hope for the best. And after all that, what do I find? Danceny has managed to hold her hand for five seconds, and when asked to let go, to Cécile's extreme annoyance, he does. You really have to put some backbone into him. Afterwards the little one said to me, 'Oh, Madame, I wish you were Danceny': and, do you know, just for a minute, I wished I was.

VALMONT: I often wonder how you managed to invent yourself.

MERTEUIL: I had no choice, did I, I'm a woman. Women are obliged to be far more skilful than men, because who ever wastes time cultivating inessential skills? You think you put as much ingenuity into winning us as we put into losing: well, it's debatable, I suppose, but from then on, you hold every ace in the pack. You can ruin us whenever the fancy takes you: all we can achieve by denouncing you is to enhance your prestige. We can't even get rid of you when we want to: we're compelled to unstitch, painstakingly, what you would just cut through. We either have to devise some way of making you want to leave us, so you'll feel too guilty to harm us; or find a reliable means of blackmail: otherwise you can destroy our reputation and our life with a few well-chosen words. So of course I had to invent: not only myself, but ways of escape no one else has ever thought of, not even I, because I had to be fast enough on my feet to know how to improvise. And I've succeeded, because I always knew I was born to dominate your sex and avenge my own.

VALMONT: Yes; but what I asked you was how.

MERTEUIL: When I came out into society I'd already realized that the role I was condemned to, namely to keep quiet and do as I was told, gave me the perfect opportunity to listen and pay attention: not to what people told me, which was naturally of no interest, but to whatever it was they were trying to hide. I practised detachment. I learned how to smile pleasantly while, under the table, I stuck a fork into the back of my hand. I became not merely impenetrable, but a virtuoso of deceit. Needless to say, at that stage nobody told me anything: and it wasn't pleasure I was after, it was knowledge. But when, in the interests of furthering that knowledge, I told my confessor I'd done 'everything', his reaction was so appalled, I began to get a sense of how extreme pleasure might be. No sooner had I made this discovery than my mother announced my marriage: so I was able to contain my curiosity and arrived in Monsieur de Merteuil's arms a virgin.

All in all, Merteuil gave me little cause for complaint: and the minute I began to find him something of a nuisance, he very tactfully died.

I used my year of mourning to complete my studies: I consulted the strictest moralists to learn how to appear; philosophers to find out what to think; and novelists to see what I could get away with. And finally I was well placed to perfect my techniques.

VALMONT: Describe them.

MERTEUIL: Only flirt with those you intend to refuse: then you acquire a reputation for invincibility, whilst slipping safely away with the lover of your choice. A poor choice is less dangerous than an obvious choice. Never write letters. Get them to write letters. Always be sure they think they're the only one. Win or die.

(VALMONT *smiles. He looks at her for a moment.*)

VALMONT: These principles are infallible, are they?

MERTEUIL: When I want a man, I have him; when he wants to tell, he finds he can't. That's the whole story.

VALMONT: And was that our story?

(MERTEUIL *pauses before answering.*)

MERTEUIL: I wanted you before we'd even met. My self-esteem demanded it. Then, when you began to pursue me . . . I wanted you so badly. It's the only one of my notions has ever got the better of me. Single combat.

VALMONT: Thank you.

(*He's about to say more, but is interrupted by the arrival of Merteuil's* MAJORDOMO, *escorting the* CHEVALIER DANCENY, *a Knight of Malta, an eager and handsome young man of about 20.* DANCENY *hurries over and bows to kiss* MERTEUIL's *hand. Then he acknowledges* VALMONT.)

DANCENY: Vicomte.

VALMONT: My dear young man. How good to see you again.

(DANCENY *turns back to* MERTEUIL, *speaks a trifle breathlessly.*)

DANCENY: I'm so sorry to be late, Madame.

MERTEUIL: Very nearly too late.

(*But looking up at his sincerely repentant expression, she softens.*)

As you know, Mademoiselle de Volanges . . .

DANCENY: It gives me such pleasure to hear her name spoken, Madame.

MERTEUIL: Yes, yes, quite. As I was saying, Mademoiselle de Volanges has done me the honour of making me her confidante and counsellor in this matter which concerns you both.

DANCENY: She could hardly have chosen more wisely.

MERTEUIL: Yes, well, be that as it may, I felt very strongly that in this situation, which is exceedingly delicate, you too might find it beneficial to be able to confide in someone sympathetic, a person of experience: and the Vicomte de Valmont, who is known to you as well as being an old

friend of mine and a man of unswerving discretion, seems
to me an ideal choice. And should you agree, he's very
kindly consented to devote himself to your interests.
(*A frown crosses* VALMONT's *face: but by the time* DANCENY,
*who for his part seems slightly flustered by this offer, turns to
him, it's vanished.*)

DANCENY: Well . . .

VALMONT: Perhaps it is my reputation which is causing you to
hesitate: if so, I think I can assure you that a man's own
mistakes are not necessarily a guide to his faculty for
objective judgement.

DANCENY: No, of course not, I certainly wouldn't have the
impudence, no, it's . . . the fact is, this is not a
conventional intrigue with the aim of . . . that's to say, my
love and respect . . .

VALMONT: We're not dealing, you mean, with a frivolous
coquette or a bored wife?

DANCENY: Precisely. A person like Mademoiselle de Volanges
must be treated with the utmost consideration. And my
own position has certain weaknesses, of which I'm only too
bitterly aware. Her great fortune, for example, compared to
my own precarious condition . . .

VALMONT: Naturally, there would be no excuse for trying to
manoeuvre her into such a pass that she would be forced to
marry you, that would be quite wrong.

DANCENY: You do understand how I feel.

MERTEUIL: Of course he does, what did I tell you?

DANCENY: You see, I'm quite happy with things as they are, as
long as she consents to see me, to continue with the music
lessons.

VALMONT: Ah, the music lessons.
(*The* MAJORDOMO *reappears and crosses the room to murmur to*
MERTEUIL. *She gives him some instructions in an undertone
and he bows and leaves.*)
In any case, I have absolutely no wish to press my
attentions on you . . .

DANCENY: No, please . . .

VALMONT: But do rest assured that I am honoured to be at your

34

disposal.

DANCENY: The honour, Monsieur, is entirely mine, and any contact with you would be a privilege. Perhaps you would care to . . .?

MERTEUIL: I'm sorry to interrupt you, Chevalier, but I'm afraid you must leave. Madame de Volanges has just been announced. You see now why I was concerned at your late arrival.

DANCENY: Maybe this would be a good opportunity for me to pay my respects and hope to . . .

MERTEUIL: I really think at this juncture, Monsieur Danceny, it would be prudent for you not to be found here. That is if you want me to be of any effective assistance in the future.

(*During this speech, a* FOOTMAN *has entered.*)

DANCENY: Of course, whatever you think fit.

MERTEUIL: Goodbye, Chevalier. My man will show you to a side exit.

(DANCENY *kisses her hand in hurried farewell.* VALMONT *takes his arm as he crosses to the door.*)

VALMONT: I have to go to Versailles tomorrow, I don't know if you'd care to accompany me.

DANCENY: I'd like that very much.

VALMONT: Good, I'll send a carriage for you at nine.

(DANCENY *vanishes with the* FOOTMAN. VALMONT *turns back to* MERTEUIL.)

So this is the scene you have planned for me?

MERTEUIL: If you'd care to go behind the screen.

(*She indicates a screen in a corner of the room, a trace of anxious impatience in her voice.*)

VALMONT: I think you might have consulted me before offering my services as general factotum to that exasperating boy. I don't find lovers' complaints remotely entertaining outside of the Opéra.

MERTEUIL: I was sure that if anyone could help him . . .

VALMONT: Help? He doesn't need help, he needs hindrances: if he has to climb over enough of them, he might inadvertently fall on top of her.

MERTEUIL: I'll see what I can do: now, Vicomte, the screen.

(VALMONT *starts moving towards it, then hesitates.*)

VALMONT: Are you sure I shouldn't confront her? Give her some evidence for those rude letters?

MERTEUIL: Quick.

(VALMONT *moves swiftly and is only just behind the screen in time not to be seen by* MME DE VOLANGES, *as she's shown in by the* MAJORDOMO. MERTEUIL, *who has assumed a grave expression, rises to greet her, kissing her on both cheeks.*)

VOLANGES: Your note said it was urgent . . .

MERTEUIL: It's days now, I haven't been able to think about anything else, I couldn't decide what to do for the best. Finally I saw there was no escaping the fact it was my plain duty to tell you. Please sit down.

(MME DE VOLANGES, *now decidedly uneasy, does so, as* MERTEUIL *paces to and fro, looking anguished.*)

As you know, in recent weeks, Cécile has been kind enough to accept my friendship and, I believe, bestow on me her own.

VOLANGES: Yes, of course, she's devoted to you.

MERTEUIL: This is what makes this duty doubly difficult to perform.

VOLANGES: This has something to do with Cécile?

MERTEUIL: I may be wrong; I pray Heaven I am.

(*She pauses again; by now,* MME DE VOLANGES *is thoroughly alarmed.*)

VOLANGES: Go on.

(MERTEUIL *takes a deep breath.*)

MERTEUIL: I have reason to believe that a, how can I describe it, a dangerous liaison has sprung up between your daughter and the Chevalier Danceny.

(*Silence.* MME DE VOLANGES *is dumbfounded and so, should he be visible behind the screen, is* VALMONT. *But it takes only a few seconds for* MME DE VOLANGES *to recover her equilibrium.*)

VOLANGES: No, no, that's completely absurd. Cécile is still a child, she understands nothing of these things; and Danceny is an entirely respectable young man.

MERTEUIL: If you were to be right, no one would be happier

than I.

VOLANGES: Naturally, they've never been together unchaperoned, generally by me and often by you.

MERTEUIL: Precisely, that's when I first formed the impression that something was passing between them: the way they looked at each other.

VOLANGES: I'm sure it's merely their feeling for the music.

MERTEUIL: Perhaps so. But there was one other thing. Tell me, does Cécile have a great many correspondents?

VOLANGES: She writes, I suppose, an average number of letters. Relatives, friends from the convent . . . Why?

MERTEUIL: I went into her room at the beginning of this week, I simply knocked and entered without waiting for a reply, and she was stuffing a letter into the left-hand drawer of her bureau, in which, I couldn't help noticing, there seemed to be a large number of similar letters.

(*Silence. Then* MME DE VOLANGES *rises to her feet.*)

VOLANGES: I'm most grateful to you. I'll see myself out.

MERTEUIL: I hope you don't think me interfering.

VOLANGES: Not at all.

MERTEUIL: And do I hope, if, God forbid, you do discover anything compromising, you won't tell Cécile it was I who was responsible. I would hate to forfeit her trust, and if there is to be a period of difficulty, I would like to think my advice might be of some use to her.

VOLANGES: Of course.

(MERTEUIL *rings.* MME DE VOLANGES *stands there, still in a state of mild shock.*)

MERTEUIL: Would you think it impertinent if I were to make another suggestion?

VOLANGES: No, no.

MERTEUIL: If my recollection is correct, I overheard you saying to the Vicomte de Valmont that his aunt had invited you to stay at her château.

VOLANGES: She has, yes, repeatedly.

MERTEUIL: A spell in the country might be the very thing until all this blows over.

VOLANGES: If what you tell me has any truth in it, I may very well send her back to the convent.

MERTEUIL: Wouldn't it be better to threaten that as a
punishment if there's any resumption of relations?

VOLANGES: Perhaps. I can't believe you're right about this.

MERTEUIL: Let's hope not.

(*The* MAJORDOMO *has arrived and* MERTEUIL *beckons him
over.* MME DE VOLANGES *meanwhile is lost in thought. She
looks up, frowning.*)

VOLANGES: Isn't the Vicomte staying there at the moment?

MERTEUIL: I understand he's returned to Paris.

(*She embraces* MME DE VOLANGES *warmly.*)

I expect I've imagined the whole thing and tomorrow we'll
be able to laugh at my stupidity. If so, I hope you'll be able
to forgive me.

VOLANGES: My dear, I shall always be more than grateful for
your concern.

(*They part; and she moves slowly out of the room, bowed down
with care, following the* MAJORDOMO. *Because of her slow
progress,* VALMONT *emerges from behind the screen before she's
disappeared, to* MERTEUIL's *alarm. But* MME DE VOLANGES
doesn't look back and VALMONT *can't resist making faces at
her retreating back, causing* MERTEUIL *to hiss at him.*)

MERTEUIL: Stop it.

VALMONT: So, you understand I've returned to Paris?

MERTEUIL: You asked for hindrances.

VALMONT: You're a genuinely wicked woman.

MERTEUIL: And you wanted a chance to make my cousin suffer.

VALMONT: I can't resist you.

MERTEUIL: I've made it easy for you.

VALMONT: But all this is most inconvenient: the Comtesse de
Beaulieu has invited me to stay.

MERTEUIL: Well, you'll have to put her off.

VALMONT: The Comtesse has promised me extensive use of her
gardens. It seems her husband's fingers are not as green as
they once were.

MERTEUIL: Maybe not. But from what I hear, all his friends are
gardeners.

VALMONT: Is that so?

MERTEUIL: You want your revenge: I want my revenge. I'm afraid there's really only one place you can go.

VALMONT: Back to Auntie, eh?

MERTEUIL: Back to Auntie. Where you can also pursue that other matter. You have some evidence to procure, have you not?

VALMONT: Don't you think it would be a generous gesture, show a proper confidence in my abilities, I mean, to take that evidence for granted, and . . . ?

MERTEUIL: I need it in writing, Vicomte.

(*He gives her his most charming smile, but it leaves her unmoved.*)

And now you must leave me.

VALMONT: Must I? Why?

MERTEUIL: Because I'm hungry.

VALMONT: Yes, I've quite an appetite myself.

MERTEUIL: Then go home and eat.

(*Silence. Then he crosses to her and lingeringly kisses her hand.*)
In writing.

(VALMONT *smiles, turns and strides away.*)

FIVE

A week later. After lunch. The salon in Mme de Rosemonde's château. MME DE TOURVEL *is stretched out on the chaise-longue, ashen;* CÉCILE *sits in the window, working at her tapestry;* MME DE ROSEMONDE *and* MME DE VOLANGES *sit at the card table; and only* VALMONT *is on his feet, moving around the room, his eye roving from* MME DE TOURVEL *to* CÉCILE *and back again.*

ROSEMONDE: You'll be pleased to hear, my dear, that Armand is on his feet again and back at work.
VALMONT: Who?
ROSEMONDE: Monsieur Armand, you remember, whose family you helped so generously.
VALMONT: Oh, yes.
   (*He comes to rest and sits down, his eye fixed now on* MME DE TOURVEL. *When she looks at him, he looks away for a few seconds at* CÉCILE, *and is gratified to notice, when he looks back at* MME DE TOURVEL, *that she's still looking at him, although she looks away again, in some confusion, the minute he catches her out.*)
ROSEMONDE: We've been keeping an eye on things while you've been away: I must say he never ceases to sing your praises.
   (*She turns to* MME DE VOLANGES.)
   When my nephew was last staying here, we discovered quite by chance that he had been down to the village and . . .
   (VALMONT *suddenly rises to his feet, still staring at* MME DE TOURVEL.)
VALMONT: Are you feeling all right, Madame?
   (*Momentary confusion.*)
   I'm sorry to interrupt you, Aunt, it seemed to me all of a sudden that Madame de Tourvel didn't look at all well.
TOURVEL: I'm . . . no, I'm quite all right.
   (*By now,* MME DE ROSEMONDE *and* MME DE VOLANGES

are on their feet and hurrying towards MME DE TOURVEL,
*who now does look genuinely ill, despite her feeble protests. As
they bear down on her,* VALMONT *turns towards* CÉCILE,
*who's still sitting, needle poised, in the window, and deftly
throws a letter into her lap. She's so amazed by this, she sits
there for a moment, gaping: until she grasps the significance of*
VALMONT'*s impatient gestures, tosses her tapestry aside and
stuffs the letter in her pocket. Finally, again at a gesture from*
VALMONT, *she moves towards the chaise-longue, exhibiting
polite concern and standing, next to* VALMONT, *at a respectful
distance from the centre of attention,* MME DE TOURVEL.)

ROSEMONDE: You do look dreadfully pale, my dear.

TOURVEL: I'm all right.

VOLANGES: Perhaps you need some air. Do you feel constricted
in any way?

TOURVEL: No, really . . .

VALMONT: I feel sure Madame de Volanges is right, as usual. A
turn around the grounds, perhaps.

ROSEMONDE: Yes, yes, a little walk in the garden, it's not too
cool, I think.

TOURVEL: Well, perhaps . . .

VOLANGES: Come along, my dear, we'll all accompany you.

TOURVEL: I'll be quite happy on my own.

VALMONT: You'll have to excuse me, ladies, but I think you're
right to insist on chaperoning Madame.

(MME DE TOURVEL *is wrong-footed by this: she frowns slightly
in puzzlement and allows a shawl to be wrapped around her
shoulders, as she's propelled towards the french windows by*
MME DE ROSEMONDE *and* MME DE VOLANGES.)

ROSEMONDE: Fresh air will do you the world of good.

VOLANGES: The meal was somewhat heavy, perhaps . . .

ROSEMONDE: I don't believe that can be the cause, Solange is
an excellent cook . . .

(*During this exchange,* CÉCILE *has gathered up her shawl and
made to follow the others. As she's spreading it across her
shoulders, however, she's startled to find it tugged away from
her by* VALMONT, *who drops it on a chair and simultaneously
murmurs to her between clenched teeth.*)

VALMONT: Come back for it.

(*She frowns at him for a moment, then follows the still-clucking ladies, who are now supporting* MME DE TOURVEL *on either side, out into the garden. Hiatus.* VALMONT *moves around the room, apparently well pleased. Presently,* CÉCILE *reappears and stands hesitantly just inside the windows.* VALMONT *picks up her shawl and strides towards her.*)

I don't want to arouse suspicion, Mademoiselle, so I must be brief and I must ask you to pay close attention to what I say. As you've no doubt guessed, the letter I gave you is from our friend, the Chevalier Danceny.

CÉCILE: Yes, I thought so, Monsieur.

VALMONT: And as I'm sure you're also aware, the handing-over of letters is a far from easy matter to accomplish. I can't very well create a diversion every day.

CÉCILE: And Maman has taken away my paper and pens.

VALMONT: Right, now listen carefully: there are two large cupboards in the antechamber next to your room. In the left-hand cupboard, you will find a supply of paper, pens and ink.

CÉCILE: Oh, thank you!

VALMONT: I suggest you return the Chevalier's letters to me, when you've read them, for safe-keeping.

CÉCILE: Must I?

VALMONT: It would be wise.

(*At this point,* VALMONT *produces a key from his waistcoat pocket.*)

Now, this key resembles the key to your bedroom, which I happen to know is kept in your mother's room, on the mantelpiece, tied with a blue ribbon. Take it, attach the blue ribbon to it and put it in the place of your bedroom key, which you will then bring to me. I'll be able to get a copy cut within two hours, I'll return you the original and you can put it back in your mother's room. Then I'll be able to collect your letters and deliver Danceny's without any complications.

(*He hands the key to* CÉCILE, *who takes it dubiously.*)

Oh, and on the shelf below the writing paper, you'll find a

feather and a small bottle of oil, so that you can oil the lock and hinges on your bedroom door.

CÉCILE: Are you sure, Monsieur, I'm not sure it would be right . . .

VALMONT: How else are we going to manage this? Your mother never lets you out of her sight. You really must trust me, my dear.

CÉCILE: Well, I know Monsieur Danceny has every confidence in you . . .

VALMONT: Believe me, Mademoiselle, if there's one thing I can't abide, it's deceitfulness. It's only my very warm friendship for Danceny which would ever make me consider such methods.

(CÉCILE *smiles uncertainly and puts the key away. She stands there, obviously racked with indecision.*)

An'd now I suggest you rejoin your mama and the others before they send out a search party.

CÉCILE: Yes, Monsieur. Thank you, Monsieur.

(*She turns and hurries back into the garden with her shawl.* VALMONT *watches her go, thoughtful.*)

VALMONT: My pleasure.

(*He moves over to an armchair and sinks into it, picks up a book from the arm of the chair, finds his place and settles to read. The lights change. It's early evening now, and* VALMONT, *still reading, looks up as* MME DE TOURVEL *comes into the room. She freezes as soon as she sees* VALMONT, *who puts down his book and rises to his feet.*)

I trust you're feeling a little better, Madame.

TOURVEL: If I had felt ill, Monsieur, it would not be difficult to guess who was responsible.

VALMONT: You can't mean me. Do you?

TOURVEL: You promised to leave here.

VALMONT: And I did.

TOURVEL: Then how can you be insensitive enough to return uninvited and without warning?

VALMONT: I find myself obliged to attend to some urgent business in the area: in which, moreover, my aunt is crucially involved.

TOURVEL: I only hope it can be dealt with promptly.

(*By now,* MME DE TOURVEL *has cautiously moved closer to the centre of the room. As the conversation continues,* VALMONT *contrives, imperceptibly, to manoeuvre himself between her and the door.*)

VALMONT: Why are you so angry with me?

TOURVEL: I'm not angry. Although, since you gave me a solemn undertaking not to offend me when you wrote and then in your very first letter spoke of nothing but the disorders of love, I'm certainly entitled to be.

VALMONT: I was away almost three weeks and wrote to you only three times. Since I was quite unable to think about anything but you, some might say I showed heroic restraint.

TOURVEL: Not in so far as you persisted in writing about your love, despite my pleas for you not to do so.

VALMONT: It's true: I couldn't find the strength to obey you.

TOURVEL: You claim to think there's some connection between what you call love and happiness: I can't believe that there is.

VALMONT: In these circumstances, I agree. When the love is unrequited . . .

TOURVEL: As it must be. You know it's impossible for me to reciprocate your feelings; and even if I did, it could only cause me suffering, without making you any the happier.

VALMONT: But what else could I have written to you about, other than my love? What else is there? I believe I've done everything you've asked of me.

TOURVEL: You've done nothing of the sort.

VALMONT: I left here when you wanted me to.

TOURVEL: And you came back.

(*Silence, as* VALMONT *searches for a way forward, momentarily at a loss.*)

I've offered you my friendship, Monsieur. It's the only thing I can give you: why can't you accept it?

VALMONT: I could pretend to: but that would be dishonest.

TOURVEL: You're not answering my question.

VALMONT: The man I used to be would have been content with friendship; and set about trying to turn it to his advantage.

44

But I've changed now: and I can't conceal from you that I love you tenderly, passionately and above all, respectfully. So how am I to demote myself to the tepid position of friend?

(VALMONT's *strategy has paid off, because at this moment* MME DE TOURVEL *decides to leave the room and finds the way blocked.*)

And in any case, you're no longer even pretending to show friendship.

TOURVEL: What do you mean?

VALMONT: Well, is this friendly?

TOURVEL: You can hardly expect me to stay here and listen to the expression of sentiments you know very well I can only find insulting.

VALMONT: I think you're misunderstanding me: I know you can bestow on me nothing more than your friendship, for which, by the way, I'm profoundly grateful. In the same way, I can feel nothing less for you than love. We both know this is the true position: can't we simply acknowledge it? I don't see why recognition of the truth should lose me your friendship. Openness and honesty scarcely deserve to be punished, don't you agree?

TOURVEL: You are adept, Monsieur, at framing questions which preclude the answer no. Your honesty or otherwise is not at issue. The point is, surely, that I was weak enough to be persuaded to grant you a favour you should never have obtained; and furthermore I did this under certain conditions, not a single one of which you have observed. Naturally, I feel you've exploited my good faith.

VALMONT: What can I say to reassure you? How can you be afraid of me when, because I love you, your happiness is far more important to me than my own? You've made me a better person: you mustn't now undo your handiwork.

TOURVEL: I've no wish to: but I must ask whether you're going to leave the room or let me pass.

VALMONT: But why?

TOURVEL: Because I find this conversation distressing. I can't seem to make you understand what I mean; and I've no

45

wish to hear what you invariably get round to saying.

VALMONT: Very well, I shall leave you in possession of the field.

TOURVEL: Thank you.

VALMONT: But look: I shall expedite my business, as you ask. But we are to be living under the same roof, at least for a few days; could we not contrive to tolerate it when fate throws us together? Surely we don't have to try to avoid each other?

(*Silence.* VALMONT *waits.*)

TOURVEL: Of course not. Providing you adhere to my few simple rules.

VALMONT: I shall obey you in this as in everything. I wish you knew me well enough to recognize how much you've changed me. My friends in Paris remarked on it at once. I've become the soul of consideration, charitable, conscientious, more celibate than a monk . . .

TOURVEL: More celibate?

VALMONT: Well, you know, the stories one hears in Paris. (*Pause.*) It's all due to your influence, I have you to thank for it. And now, good evening.

(*He bows deep and turns away, begins moving towards the door.*)

TOURVEL: Monsieur . . . ?

VALMONT: What?

(*She looks at him for a moment, troubled: then shakes her head.*)

TOURVEL: Nothing.

(VALMONT *turns away, permits himself a private smile and leaves.* MME DE TOURVEL *stands for a long time, not moving, locked in some personal struggle.*)

SIX

A fortnight later. The middle of the night. Cécile's bedroom in the château. Darkness. CÉCILE *is fast asleep. After a while, there's the sound of a key in the lock. It operates smoothly and* VALMONT *lets himself quietly into the room. He's wearing a dressing-gown and carrying a dark-lantern. He crosses to the bed and stands for a moment, contemplating the still-sleeping* CÉCILE. *He puts the lantern down carefully and, after some thought, leans forward and very gently eases back the covers. Disturbed, she stirs but still doesn't wake.* VALMONT *puts a hand across her mouth. Her eyes open, wide and staring.* VALMONT *smiles down at her and speaks in a whisper.*

VALMONT: Nothing to worry about.
  (*He removes his hand; she continues to gape at him.*)
CÉCILE: Have you . . . have you brought a letter?
VALMONT: No. Oh, no.
CÉCILE: Then what . . . ?
  (*Instead of answering, he leans over to kiss her. There's a brief, fierce struggle, in which* CÉCILE *successfully defends herself from the kiss, but is taken entirely by surprise when* VALMONT *plunges a hand up inside her nightdress. Her eyes widen in horror, but her cry is instantly stifled as* VALMONT's *other hand clamps down on her mouth. She writhes determinedly for a moment, succeeds in freeing her head and dives across the bed to reach for the bell-pull.* VALMONT *dives on to the bed in his turn, grasping her wrist just in time. They grapple fiercely and silently for a moment, until he manages to subdue her.*)
VALMONT: You mustn't do that. What are you going to tell your mother when she arrives? How will you explain the fact that I have your key? If I tell her I'm here at your invitation, I have a feeling she'll believe me.
  (*His hand is back in position now, and they're lying side by side on the bed.*)
CÉCILE: What do you want?
VALMONT: Well, I don't know, what do you think?

47

CÉCILE: No, please, don't. Please.

VALMONT: All right. I just want you to give me a kiss.

CÉCILE: A kiss?

VALMONT: That's all.

CÉCILE: And then will you go?

VALMONT: Then I'll go.

CÉCILE: Promise?

VALMONT: Whatever you say.

(CÉCILE *flops back on the pillow, with a slight groan and speaks, almost inaudibly.*)

CÉCILE: All right.

(*Without removing his hand,* VALMONT *leans over her and gives her a long kiss. After a while he pulls away, but makes no move to disengage himself further.*)

All right?

VALMONT: Very nice.

CÉCILE: No, I mean, will you go now?

VALMONT: Oh, I don't think so.

CÉCILE: But you promised.

VALMONT: I promised to go when you gave me a kiss. You didn't give me a kiss. I gave you a kiss. Not the same thing at all.

(*Silence.* CÉCILE *peers at him miserably. He looks back at her, calmly waiting.*)

CÉCILE: And if I give you a kiss . . . ?

VALMONT: That's what I said.

CÉCILE: You really promise?

VALMONT: Let's just get ourselves more comfortable, shall we?

CÉCILE: Do you?

(VALMONT *disposes the cover over them, then leans back to look down on her. He replaces his hand and* CÉCILE *reacts with a start.*)

Please don't do that.

VALMONT: I'll take it away. After the kiss.

CÉCILE: Promise?

VALMONT: Yes, yes.

CÉCILE: Swear?

VALMONT: I swear. Now put your arms round me.

48

(CÉCILE *gives him a long, surprisingly intense kiss, her eyes tightly closed. Suddenly, she pulls away from him as much as she can, her eyes now wide with amazement.* VALMONT's *hand comes slowly up from under the cover.* CÉCILE *continues to look appalled.*)
See. I told you I'd take my hand away.

SEVEN

It's the following day, 1 October. The low afternoon sun slants in through the windows of the salon in Mme de Rosemonde's château. At first, the room is empty: then CÉCILE *appears, arm-in-arm with* MME DE MERTEUIL *who seems almost to be supporting her.* CÉCILE *looks exhausted and distraught;* MERTEUIL, *solicitous.*

MERTEUIL: My dear, I really can't help you unless you tell me what's troubling you.

CÉCILE: I can't, I just can't.

MERTEUIL: I thought we'd agreed not to keep any secrets from one another.

CÉCILE: I'm so unhappy.
> (*She bursts into tears.* MERTEUIL *takes her in her arms and soothes her mechanically, her expression, as long as it's not seen by* CÉCILE, *bored and impatient.*)
> Everything's gone wrong since the day Maman found Danceny's letters.

MERTEUIL: Yes, that was very stupid of you. How could you have let that happen?

CÉCILE: Someone must have told her, she went straight to my bureau and opened the drawer I was keeping them in.

MERTEUIL: Who could have done such a thing?

CÉCILE: It must have been my chambermaid . . .

MERTEUIL: Or your confessor perhaps?

CÉCILE: Oh, no, surely not.

MERTEUIL: You can't always trust those people, my dear.

CÉCILE: That's terrible.

MERTEUIL: But today, what is the matter today?

CÉCILE: You'll be angry with me.

MERTEUIL: Are you sure you don't want me to be angry with you?
> (CÉCILE *looks up at* MERTEUIL, *surprised by the acuteness of this idea.*)
> Come along.

CÉCILE: I don't know how to speak the words.

MERTEUIL: Perhaps I am beginning to get angry.

(She's spoken quietly; and now there's a long silence. Finally, CÉCILE *takes a deep breath.)*

CÉCILE: Last night . . .

MERTEUIL: Yes.

CÉCILE: So that we could exchange letters to and from Danceny without arousing suspicion, I gave Monsieur de Valmont the key to my bedroom . . .

MERTEUIL: Yes.

CÉCILE: And last night he used it. I thought he'd just come to bring me a letter. But he hadn't. And by the time I realized what he had come for, it was, well, it was too late to stop him . . .

(She bursts into tears again; but this time MERTEUIL *doesn't take her in her arms. Instead, she considers her coolly for a moment before speaking.)*

MERTEUIL: You mean to tell me you're upset because Monsieur de Valmont has taught you something you've undoubtedly been dying to learn?

*(*CÉCILE's *tears are cut off and she looks up in shock.)*

CÉCILE: What?

MERTEUIL: And am I to understand that what generally brings a girl to her senses has deprived you of yours?

CÉCILE: I thought you'd be horrified.

MERTEUIL: Tell me: you resisted him, did you?

CÉCILE: Of course I did, as much as I could.

MERTEUIL: But he forced you?

CÉCILE: It wasn't that exactly, but I found it almost impossible to defend myself.

MERTEUIL: Why was that? Did he tie you up?

CÉCILE: No, no, but he has a way of putting things, you just can't think of an answer.

MERTEUIL: Not even no?

CÉCILE: I kept saying no, all the time: but somehow that wasn't what I was doing. And in the end . . .

MERTEUIL: Yes?

CÉCILE: I told him he could come back tonight.

(*Silence.* CÉCILE *seems, once again, trembling on the edge of tears.*)

I'm so ashamed.

MERTEUIL: You'll find the shame is like the pain: you only feel it once.

CÉCILE: And this morning it was terrible. As soon as I saw Maman, I couldn't help it, I burst into tears.

MERTEUIL: I'm surprised you missed the opportunity to bring the whole thing to a rousing climax by confessing all. You wouldn't be worrying about tonight if you'd done that; you'd be packing your bags for the convent.

CÉCILE: What am I going to do?

MERTEUIL: You really want my advice?

CÉCILE: Please.

(MERTEUIL *considers a moment.*)

MERTEUIL: Allow Monsieur de Valmont to continue your instruction. Convince your mother you have forgotten Danceny. And raise no objection to the marriage.

(CÉCILE *gapes at her, bewildered.*)

CÉCILE: With Monsieur de Gercourt?

MERTEUIL: When it comes to marriage one man is as good as the next; and even the least accommodating is less trouble than a mother.

CÉCILE: But what about Danceny?

MERTEUIL: He seems patient enough; and once you're married, you should be able to see him without undue difficulty.

CÉCILE: I thought you once said to me, I'm sure you did, one evening at the Opéra, that once I was married, I would have to be faithful to my husband.

MERTEUIL: Your mind must have been wandering, you must have been listening to the opera.

CÉCILE: So, are you saying I'm going to have to do that with three different men?

MERTEUIL: I'm saying, you stupid little girl, that provided you take a few elementary precautions, you can do it, or not, with as many men as you like, as often as you like, in as many different ways as you like. Our sex has few enough advantages, you may as well make the most of those you have. Now here comes your mama, so remember what I've said and, above all, no more snivelling.

CÉCILE: Yes, Madame.

(*And by now,* MME DE VOLANGES *is more or less upon them. She acknowledges* MERTEUIL *perfunctorily, but her anxious attention is directed almost entirely towards* CÉCILE, *whose expression is now profoundly thoughtful.*)

VOLANGES: How are you feeling now, my dear?

CÉCILE: Oh, much better, thank you, Maman.

VOLANGES: You look so tired. I think you should go to bed.

CÉCILE: No, really, I've . . .

MERTEUIL: I think you should do as your mother suggests. We can arrange for something to be brought to your room. I'm sure it would do you good.

CÉCILE: Well. Perhaps you're right, Madame.

(*She curtsies to* MERTEUIL *and kisses her mother on both cheeks.*)

VOLANGES: I'll come up and see you later on.

(CÉCILE *makes a demure exit, watched by the others. When she's left the room,* MME DE VOLANGES *turns back to* MERTEUIL.)

You have such a very good influence on her.

MERTEUIL: I like to think so. But what do you suppose is the matter?

VOLANGES: Didn't she tell you?

MERTEUIL: No, we merely spoke of how she was enjoying the country.

VOLANGES: That makes me even more certain of the cause of her unhappiness. She's pining for that young man. I'm afraid it's beginning to affect her health.

MERTEUIL: Do you think so?

VOLANGES: This morning, I simply asked her how she'd slept, and she threw herself into my arms and cried and cried.

(MME DE VOLANGES *sighs deeply. Then she turns decisively to* MERTEUIL.)

My dear, I'd be very grateful if you would allow me to discuss this with you seriously. I've been brooding about it all day, and now I really feel I need your advice.

MERTEUIL: My dear friend, please, I'd be proud to think I

53

could be of any help to you.

VOLANGES: Well. I've been reconsidering. I really think perhaps I should break off Cécile's engagement with Monsieur de Gercourt.

(MERTEUIL's *head jerks up*.)

He is no doubt a better match than Danceny, but the family, after all, is not decisively superior. Danceny is not rich, of course: but I dare say Cécile is rich enough for both of them. And the most important thing is that they love each other. Don't you agree?

(*Silence*. MERTEUIL *is thinking fast*.)

You think I'm wrong?

MERTEUIL: I have every confidence that your eventual decision will be the right one. If I were able to take a more objective view of the situation, it would only be because, in this case, I am not affected by the altogether praiseworthy emotion of maternal love.

VOLANGES: Please go on, I do rely on your judgement.

MERTEUIL: Well. It seems to me a question of distinguishing what's correct from what's pleasurable. To say this young man is entitled to your daughter just because of his passion for her is a little like saying a thief is entitled to your money. I'm not at all sure how appropriate an emotion love is, particularly within marriage. I believe friendship, trust and mutual respect are infinitely more important.

VOLANGES: And you don't approve of Danceny?

MERTEUIL: There's no denying that, as suitors, there can be no comparison between them. I know money isn't everything: but will sixty thousand a year really be sufficient to maintain the kind of establishment Cécile will be obliged to run, even as Madame Danceny? Of course, I wouldn't dream of suggesting in any way that Danceny has allowed himself to be influenced by financial considerations . . .

VOLANGES: But?

MERTEUIL: Precisely.

(*Silence*. MME DE VOLANGES *reflects*.)

But, as I say, this is only an opinion. Naturally, it's your decision.

54

VOLANGES: Yes.

MERTEUIL: Perhaps you ought not to take it on the strength of a single outburst, which might have any number of, well, medical explanations, for example.

VOLANGES: Perhaps you're right.

MERTEUIL: In any event, I hope we can discuss it further when we're all back in Paris.

(*She accompanies this remark with a gesture which alerts* MME DE VOLANGES *to the fact that* VALMONT *has entered the room.* VALMONT *bows, as the ladies turn to him.*)

VALMONT: Mesdames.

VOLANGES: If you'll excuse me, Monsieur, I must go and make arrangements for some supper to be taken up to my daughter.

VALMONT: Oh, is she indisposed?

VOLANGES: For the moment.

VALMONT: The young have such miraculous powers of recuperation. I'm sure she'll soon be back in the saddle. Tell her I hope so, at least.

VOLANGES: Thank you, Monsieur.

(*She leaves the room briskly.* VALMONT *watches her go and then turns back to grin at* MERTEUIL.)

VALMONT: You see, she can hardly bear to be in the same room with me.

MERTEUIL: But I gather you've had your revenge. Well done.

VALMONT: So you know?

MERTEUIL: The little one could hardly wait to tell me.

VALMONT: A favourable report, I trust?

MERTEUIL: On the contrary, Vicomte, if I hadn't spoken to her sharply, I think on your next visit you'd have found her door bolted as well as locked.

VALMONT: You surprise me. I was malicious enough to use no more strength than could easily be resisted.

MERTEUIL: Still, for some reason she seems to think it was rather an underhand approach.

VALMONT: I'd been postponing it, to tell you the truth. But when I heard you were expected today, I wanted to be able to afford you some amusement at least.

MERTEUIL: It's just as well I did decide to look in, because, as it turns out, your initiative came within an ace of sabotaging our whole plan.

VALMONT: What do you mean?

MERTEUIL: Madame de Volanges was so concerned about Cécile's appearance this morning, she resolved to allow her to marry Danceny after all.

VALMONT: No.

MERTEUIL: I think I've been able to talk her out of it: but the fact remains, you almost lost us our revenge on Gercourt.

VALMONT: I could hardly be expected to anticipate this sudden access of compassion. After all, to my knowledge, Mother Volanges has never shown signs of it before.

MERTEUIL: I'm beginning to have my doubts about you, Vicomte. Do you really deserve your reputation? You see, the real reason I consented to spend a night at this lugubrious address was that I was hoping to be shown some tear-stained bit of paper.

VALMONT: Ah.

MERTEUIL: But I can only assume from what you've been saying that no such document exists.

VALMONT: No.

MERTEUIL: Probably just as well, no doubt you're exhausted after last night's exertions.

VALMONT: I think you know me better than that.

MERTEUIL: Well, I wonder. Can you account for this extraordinary dilatoriness?

VALMONT: Lugubrious or not, I haven't experienced a moment's boredom in all the weeks I've spent here. I appreciate you may have excellent reasons for your impatience, but you mustn't try to deprive me of my simple pleasures. I've explained to you before how much I enjoy watching the battle between love and virtue.

MERTEUIL: What concerns me is that you appear to enjoy watching it more than you used to enjoy winning it.

VALMONT: All in good time.

MERTEUIL: The century is drawing to its close, Vicomte.

VALMONT: It's true that she's resisted me for more than two months now; and that's very nearly a record. But I really don't want to hurry things. We go for a walk together almost every day: a little further every time down the path that has no turning. She's accepted my love; I've accepted her friendship; we're both aware how little there is to choose between them. Her eyes are closing. Every step she tries to take away from the inevitable conclusion brings her a little nearer to it. Hopes and fears, passion and suspense: even if you were in the theatre, what more could you ask?

MERTEUIL: An audience?

VALMONT: But you: you're my audience. And when Gercourt is married and Madame de Tourvel eventually collapses, we shall tell everyone, shall we not? And the story will spread much faster than the plot of the latest play; and I've no doubt it will be much better received.

MERTEUIL: I hope you're right, Vicomte, I wish I could share your confidence.

VALMONT: I'm only sorry our agreement does not relate to the task you set me rather than the task I set myself.

MERTEUIL: I am grateful, of course: but that would have been almost insultingly simple. One does not applaud the tenor for clearing his throat.

VALMONT: You're right, how could one possibly compare them . . . ?

(*He breaks off as* MME DE ROSEMONDE *comes into the room, followed by* MME DE TOURVEL. MME DE ROSEMONDE *bustles over to* MERTEUIL *to embrace her:* MERTEUIL *responds convincingly, but it's clear she has immediately registered the look which passes between* VALMONT *and* MME DE TOURVEL, *a look that indicates that there has indeed been some progress in their relationship.*)

ROSEMONDE: I'm so delighted you could manage to visit us, my dear, even if only for such a short time.

MERTEUIL: I wish I could stay longer, Madame, but my husband's estate . . .

ROSEMONDE: Do you know, I was thinking yesterday, it's more than five years since you were last here, with your dear husband. Such a kind and such a vigorous man, who could have imagined . . . ah, well . . .

57

(MERTEUIL, *who is centrally placed, has been watching* MME DE TOURVEL *and, more particularly,* VALMONT, *who really is lost in contemplation of* MME DE TOURVEL. *She doesn't like what she sees: it clearly troubles her, even though, after only the briefest pause, she manages a civil reply to* MME DE ROSEMONDE.)

MERTEUIL: Yes, Madame, there's no denying that life is frighteningly unpredictable.

EIGHT

Two nights later. Valmont's bedroom in the château. It's empty at the moment, a couple of candles casting a dim glow. Presently, VALMONT *appears, with his dark-lantern, escorting* CÉCILE *into the room. They're both wearing dressing-gowns.* CÉCILE *looks around the room a trifle apprehensively.*

VALMONT: Much the same as your room, you see; but here, you'll be able to make as much noise as you like.
   (*He's reached the bed and presses down on the mattress.*)
   And the mattress is a little harder.
CÉCILE: Is that good?
VALMONT: Yes, that's very good.
   (CÉCILE *gives a whoop, throws off her dressing-gown and jumps on to the bed. She bounces up and down for a moment, then dives in between the sheets.* VALMONT *stands, looking down at her.*)
CÉCILE: Come on.
   (*By way of answer,* VALMONT *stretches out on the bed comfortably, his hands behind his head.*)
VALMONT: The first thing you must learn is that there is no necessity whatsoever for haste.
   (*He reaches out to caress her.*)
   Now. As with every other science, the first principle is to make sure you call everything by its proper name.
CÉCILE: I don't see why you have to talk at all.
VALMONT: Without the correct polite vocabulary, how can you indicate what you would like me to do or make me an offer of something I might find agreeable?
CÉCILE: Surely you just say . . .
VALMONT: You see, if I do my work adequately, I would like to think you'll be able to surprise Monsieur de Gercourt on your wedding night.
CÉCILE: Would he be pleased?
VALMONT: Well, of course, he'll merely assume your mama has

done her duty and fully briefed you.

(CÉCILE *bursts out laughing*.)

CÉCILE: Maman couldn't possibly talk about anything of the sort.

VALMONT: I can't think why. She was, after all, at one time, one of the most notorious young women in Paris.

CÉCILE: Maman?

VALMONT: Certainly. More noted for her enthusiasm than her ability, if I remember rightly, but none the less renowned. There was a famous occasion, oh, before you were born, this would have been, when she went to stay with the Comtesse de Beaulieu, who tactfully gave her a room between your father's and that of a Monsieur de Vressac, who was her acknowledged lover at the time. Yet in spite of these careful arrangements, she contrived to spend the night with a third party.

(CÉCILE *laughs again*.)

CÉCILE: I can't believe that; it's just gossip.

VALMONT: No, no, I assure you it's true.

CÉCILE: How do you know?

VALMONT: This third party was myself.

(CÉCILE's *jaw drops. For a moment she stares at* VALMONT, *horrified. He returns a bland smile and, all of a sudden, she can't resist smiling herself.* VALMONT *turns back the covers.*)

Well, we can return to this subject later. During the intervals. You asked me if Monsieur de Gercourt would be pleased with your abilities; and the answer is that even if he isn't, I don't believe it would be difficult to find others who would. Education is never a waste.

(*He reaches out and puts a hand round her head, drawing her to him.*)

Now. I think we might begin with one or two Latin terms.

NINE

Late the following evening. MME DE TOURVEL *lingers alone in the salon in the château. The card table is out, still scattered with cards.* MME DE TOURVEL, *drifting somewhat aimlessly, glancing at the door from time to time, seems to have no particular reason for being in the room. She starts however and moves briskly to the table to begin tidying away the cards as soon as* VALMONT, *looking elegant but frail, appears in the doorway.*

VALMONT: You're alone, Madame.
> (*He advances into the room as* MME DE TOURVEL *answers shakily.*)

TOURVEL: The others have all decided on an early night. Mademoiselle de Volanges in particular seems to be quite exhausted.

VALMONT: I must admit to being rather tired myself.
> (*He arrives at the card table.*)
> May I help you with these?
> (*He reaches for some cards, brushing her hand in the process, causing her to let go of the cards she's already collected.*)

TOURVEL: No, I'm sure the servants will . . .
> (*She moves away from the table in some confusion, heading in the general direction of the chaise-longue.* VALMONT *watches her.*)

VALMONT: I'm glad to have found you, I very much missed our walk today.

TOURVEL: Yes . . .

VALMONT: I fear with the weather as it is, we can look forward to very few more of them.

TOURVEL: This heavy rain is surely exceptional.

VALMONT: But in a week I shall have concluded my business.

TOURVEL: I see.
> (*She stops, affected by this news.* VALMONT *begins, very gradually, to move closer.*)

VALMONT: I may, however, be unable to bring myself to leave.

(MME DE TOURVEL *turns to face him, beset by conflicting emotions*.)

TOURVEL: Oh, please. You must!

VALMONT: Are you still so anxious to get rid of me?

TOURVEL: You know the answer to that. I must rely on your integrity and generosity. I want to be able to be grateful to you.

VALMONT: Forgive me if I say I don't want your gratitude. Gratitude I can get from strangers; what I want from you is something altogether deeper.

TOURVEL: I know God is punishing me for my pride. I was so certain nothing like this could ever happen to me.

VALMONT: Nothing like what?

TOURVEL: I can't . . .

VALMONT: Do you mean love? Is love what you mean?
(*He's beside her now and takes her hand. She starts, but does not remove her hand*.)

TOURVEL: Don't ask me, you promised not to speak of it.

VALMONT: But I must know. I need this consolation at least.
(*Silence.* MME DE TOURVEL *still holds* VALMONT's *hand, but cannot bring herself to look at him.* VALMONT, *meanwhile, darts a quick glance at the chaise-longue*.)

TOURVEL: I can't . . . don't you see? . . . it's impossible . . .

VALMONT: Of course I understand, I don't want you to say anything, but I must know, I must know if you love me, don't speak, you don't have to speak, I just want you to look at me. Just look. That's all I ask.
(*Long silence. Then, slowly,* MME DE TOURVEL *raises her eyes to his*.)

TOURVEL: Yes.
(*They're motionless for a moment. Then* VALMONT *releases her hand and raises his arms to embrace her. As he does so, her eyes suddenly go dead and she collapses sideways, obliging him to catch her. She sways in his arms for a moment, then comes to and jerks violently away from him. Then she bursts into tears. She stands for a moment, sobbing wildly, then rushes at* VALMONT, *falls to her knees and throws her arms round his legs*.)
For God's sake, you must leave me, if you don't want to kill

me, you must help, it's killing me!

(VALMONT, *somewhat taken aback at first by her intensity, collects himself and lifts her to her feet. For a moment they sway together in an ungainly embrace; then* MME DE TOURVEL's *sobs cease abruptly and give way to chattering teeth and almost epileptic convulsions. Startled,* VALMONT *gathers her up in his arms and carries her over to the chaise-longue where he deposits her gently. The convulsions continue, her teeth are clenched now, the blood drained from her face. He leans forward to loosen her bodice as she stares helplessly up at him. He pauses for a moment, looking down at her, as her features return to normal. They look at each other. Something passes between them; and this time it's* VALMONT *who looks away, something almost like shame darkening his expression.* MME DE TOURVEL *begins to go into shock again; and* VALMONT *breaks away and runs over to the door, shouting.*)

VALMONT: Adèle!

(*He leaves the room; and a moment later, his voice is heard.*)

(*Off*) Fetch Madame. Madame de Tourvel has been taken ill.

(*He hurries back into the room and over to the chaise-longue. As he arrives there,* MME DE TOURVEL *reaches a hand up towards him. He takes it between both of his. He looks perplexed. He stands in silence, thoughtful, massaging her hand in his. Presently,* MME DE ROSEMONDE *appears, shepherded by her* MAID. *She clucks anxiously and hurries over towards the chaise-longue.* VALMONT *releases* MME DE TOURVEL's *hand.*)
She seemed to be having difficulty breathing.

ROSEMONDE: Oh, my dear, whatever is it?

(MME DE TOURVEL *stirs, managing a faint smile.*)

TOURVEL: It's all right, I'm all right now.

VALMONT: I shall leave her in your capable hands, Aunt. Send Adèle for me if I can be of any further assistance.

(*And, still looking strangely abashed, he leaves the room.*)

ROSEMONDE: We must send for a doctor, my dear.

(MME DE TOURVEL *is roused from her rapt contemplation of* VALMONT's *departure.*)

TOURVEL: No, no please, I don't need a doctor, I'm perfectly

63

all right now.

ROSEMONDE: We mustn't take any chances.

TOURVEL: No, I just . . . I must talk to you for a moment.

(MME DE ROSEMONDE *frowns, but without surprise. She turns to gesture at the* MAID. *The* MAID *curtsies and leaves.* MME DE TOURVEL *motions* MME DE ROSEMONDE *to approach.*)

TOURVEL: Come and sit by me. I can't speak very loud. What I have to say is too difficult.

(MME DE ROSEMONDE *perches on the edge of the chaise-longue looking down at her.* MME DE TOURVEL *takes her hands.*)

I have to leave this house first thing in the morning. I'm most desperately in love.

(MME DE ROSEMONDE, *still unsurprised, bows her head.*)

To leave here is the last thing in the world I want to do: but I'd rather die than have to live with the guilt. I don't mind if I die: to live without him is going to be no life at all. But that's what I have to do. Can you understand what I'm saying?

ROSEMONDE: Of course. My dear girl. None of this is any surprise to me. The only thing which might surprise one is how little the world changes. Of course you must leave if you feel it's the right thing to do.

TOURVEL: And what should I do then? What's your advice?

ROSEMONDE: If I remember rightly, in such matters all advice is useless. You can't speak to the patient in the grip of a fever. We must talk again when you're closer to recovery.

TOURVEL: I've never been so unhappy.

ROSEMONDE: I'm sorry to say this: but those who are most worthy of love are never made happy by it. You're too young to have understood that.

TOURVEL: But why, why should that be?

ROSEMONDE: Do you still think men love the way we do? No. Men enjoy the happiness they feel; we can only enjoy the happiness we give. They're not capable of devoting themselves exclusively to one person. So to hope to be made happy by love is a certain cause of grief. I'm devoted to my nephew, but what is true of most men is doubly so of him.

TOURVEL: And yet . . . he could have . . . just now. He took pity on me, I saw it happen, I saw his decision not to take advantage of me.

ROSEMONDE: If he has released you, my dear child, it's because your example over these last few weeks has genuinely affected and improved him. If he's let you go, you must go.

TOURVEL: I will. I will.

(*She starts crying again and twists round, letting her head drop into* MME DE ROSEMONDE's *lap.* MME DE ROSEMONDE *sits, looking down, stroking* MME DE TOURVEL's *hair.*)

ROSEMONDE: There. And even if you had given way, my dear girl, God knows how hard you've struggled against it. There now.

(*She strokes her hair, as the lights fade to black.*)

ACT II

TEN

Late October. The principal salon in le Vicomte de Valmont's Paris hôtel. VALMONT *sits at his desk, writing. He signs with a flourish and looks up as* AZOLAN *appears in the doorway and hurries into the room, pausing only to bow deeply.*

VALMONT: Well, what treasures do you have in store for me today?

(AZOLAN *hands him two letters, one sealed and one unsealed.*)

AZOLAN: A letter to Madame your aunt, sir. And this one, which Julie managed to get to before it was sealed up, to Madame's confessor.

VALMONT: Ah, very good!

(*He runs an eye quickly over the contents of the letter, then proceeds to seal it and his own letter as he speaks.*)

This is excellent, I have a letter for Father Anselme myself; you may deliver them both when you leave.

AZOLAN: Yes, sir.

(*He takes the letters from* VALMONT.)

VALMONT: And what news?

AZOLAN: No visitors: there still hasn't been a single visitor since she got back from the country. Kept to her room. Bit of soup last night, but didn't touch the pheasant. Afterwards a cup of tea. Nothing else to report. Oh, yes, there is. You wanted to know what she was reading. She has two books by her bed.

VALMONT: I don't suppose you found out what they were?

AZOLAN: Course I did, sir, what do you take me for? Let me think, now. One was *Christian Thoughts*, volume two. And the other was a novel written by some Englishman. *Clarissa*.

VALMONT: Ah.

AZOLAN: See, I was right, wasn't I, sir, there was no need for me to join her staff, now was there? I can find out everything you want to know, no trouble at all.

VALMONT: I just thought you might prefer to be paid two salaries. As at the time of the Duchesse.

AZOLAN: Oh, well, sir, with Madame the Duchesse, that was quite different, I didn't mind that at all. But I couldn't wear a magistrate's livery, could I, sir, now be fair, not after being in your service.

(*He indicates his magnificent* chasseur's *uniform.* VALMONT *smiles, shaking his head. Then he opens a drawer and hands him a small bag of money.*)

Thank you, sir, thank you very much. One day I'll start saving a bit, like you recommended, but I do like to do justice to you.

VALMONT: After letting Madame de Tourvel leave my aunt's house without even managing to warn me, you're lucky to be working for anybody.

AZOLAN: Now we've been through all that, sir, haven't we? Not even Julie knew she was going till she went.

VALMONT: How is Julie?

AZOLAN: Seems a bit keener than she was in the country.

VALMONT: And yourself?

(AZOLAN *shakes his head gloomily.*)

AZOLAN: Talk about devotion to duty.

(VALMONT *smiles and looks up as a* FOOTMAN *shows* MME DE MERTEUIL *and* DANCENY *into the room. He rises to greet them, dismissing* AZOLAN *as he does so, speaking out of the corner of his mouth.*)

VALMONT: Off you go. Keep it up.

(AZOLAN *bows and leaves, together with the* FOOTMAN.)

Madame. My dear boy.

(DANCENY *embraces* VALMONT *impulsively.*)

DANCENY: Thank you, Monsieur, for everything.

(VALMONT *holds him for a moment, smiling wickedly at* MERTEUIL *over* DANCENY's *shoulder.*)

VALMONT: I was afraid I'd been a sad disappointment to you.

DANCENY: Of course I'm disappointed not to have seen Cécile for more than a month, but I believe I have you to thank for keeping our love alive.

VALMONT: Oh, as to love, she thinks of little else.

DANCENY: I had so hoped you'd be able to arrange a meeting between us in the country.

VALMONT: Well, so had I, I made all the necessary arrangements, but she was adamant.

DANCENY: I know, she said in her last letter you'd been trying hard to persuade her.

VALMONT: I did what I could. In many respects I've found her very open to persuasion, but not, alas, on this issue.

DANCENY: Yes, she said I couldn't do more myself than you've been doing on my behalf.

VALMONT: She's a most generous girl.

MERTEUIL: What else did she say?

DANCENY: She said she'd seen signs of a change of heart in her mother. Perhaps in the end she'll come round to the idea of our marriage.

MERTEUIL: That would be wonderful.

DANCENY: Anyway, how is she, that's what I've really come round to ask you, Monsieur.

VALMONT: Blooming. I really think the country air has done her good, I think she's even begun to fill out a little.

DANCENY: Really?

VALMONT: And of course she sends you all her love. She and her mother will be returning to Paris in about a fortnight, by which time the situation should be resolved one way or the other; and either way, she's longing to see you.

DANCENY: I don't know how I can bear to go another two weeks without seeing her.

MERTEUIL: We shall have to do our very best to provide some distraction for you.

DANCENY: Without your friendship and encouragement, I can't think what would have become of me.

MERTEUIL: My dear, if you'd be so kind as to wait in the carriage for a few minutes, there's a matter I must discuss with the Vicomte in private.

DANCENY: Of course.

(*He bows to* VALMONT *and pumps his hand heartily*.)

I don't know how I can ever repay you.

VALMONT: Don't give it another thought, it's been delightful.

(DANCENY *smiles charmingly at them both and leaves the room. As soon as he's gone,* VALMONT *and* MERTEUIL *burst out laughing and fall into each other's arms. They embrace for a moment and then pull apart, still smiling.*)
Poor boy. He's quite harmless.

MERTEUIL: Well, I must say, I thought Cécile's letter sounded unusually witty.

VALMONT: So I should hope: I dictated it.

MERTEUIL: Ah, Vicomte, I do adore you.

VALMONT: I have a piece of news I hope you might find entertaining: I have reason to believe the next head of the house of Gercourt might be a Valmont.

MERTEUIL: What do you mean?

VALMONT: Cécile is two weeks late.

(MERTEUIL *is startled by this: she frowns, assessing its implications.*)
Aren't you pleased?

MERTEUIL: I'm not sure. You have rather overstepped your brief.

VALMONT: Providing they hold the wedding before the end of the year, I don't see what harm can come of it.

MERTEUIL: No, you're right, the situation does have possibilities. It just makes everything a good deal more chancy. You've used no precautions, then?

VALMONT: I've tried to give her a thorough grounding in all aspects of our subject: but in this one area, I'm afraid I may have misled her to some extent.

(MERTEUIL *shakes her head, amused but still dubious.*)
Your aim was to revenge yourself on Gercourt: I've provided him with a wife trained by me to perform quite naturally services you would hesitate to request from a professional. And very likely pregnant as well. What more do you want?

MERTEUIL: All right, Vicomte, I agree, you've more than done your duty. Shame you let the other one slip through your fingers. I can only assume that's what happened?

(VALMONT'S *expression darkens.*)

VALMONT: I let her go. Can you imagine? I took pity on her.

69

She was ready, the die was cast and the bill was paid. And I relented. And, what do you know, she vanished, like a thief in the night.

MERTEUIL: Why did you let her escape?

VALMONT: I was . . . moved.

MERTEUIL: Oh, well, then, no wonder you bungled it.

VALMONT: I had no idea she was capable of being so devious.

MERTEUIL: Poor woman, what else could you expect? To surrender and not be taken, it would try the patience of a saint.

VALMONT: It won't happen again.

MERTEUIL: What you mean is, you won't get the chance again.

VALMONT: Oh, yes, this time I have a foolproof plan.

MERTEUIL: What, another one?

VALMONT: Absolutely guaranteed. I have an appointment to visit her at her house on Thursday. And this time, I shall be merciless. I'm going to punish her.

MERTEUIL: I'm pleased to hear it.

VALMONT: Why do you suppose we only feel compelled to chase the ones who run away?

MERTEUIL: Immaturity?

VALMONT: I shan't have a moment's peace until it's over, you know. I love her, I hate her, I'm furious with her, my life's a misery; I've got to have her so that I can pass all these feelings on to her and be rid of them.

(MERTEUIL *is beginning to look displeased. There's a pause, during which* VALMONT *notices this and does his best to break the mood.*)

Now tell me what's happening in your life.

MERTEUIL: Belleroche is about to fall by the wayside.

VALMONT: But this is excellent.

MERTEUIL: I have smothered him with so much affection, the poor man can hardly stand up. He's desperately trying to devise some graceful exit.

VALMONT: Long overdue, in my opinion.

MERTEUIL: And his successor has already been marked out.

VALMONT: Oh? Who's the lucky man?

(*Silence.* MERTEUIL *considers.*)

70

MERTEUIL: I'm not sure I care to tell you just at the moment.

VALMONT: Oh, well, in that case, I shall have to conceal from you the details of my foolproof plan.

MERTEUIL: That seems an acceptable enough bargain.

(VALMONT *frowns, puzzled.*)

VALMONT: What's the matter?

MERTEUIL: Nothing. I think I may have kept our young friend waiting long enough.

VALMONT: I shall call on you sometime soon after Thursday.

MERTEUIL: Only if you succeed, Vicomte. I'm not sure I could face another catalogue of incompetence.

VALMONT: Oh, I shall succeed.

MERTEUIL: I hope so. Once upon a time you were a man to be reckoned with.

(*He makes to embrace her, but she limits herself to delivering a frosty peck on the cheek and hurries away.* VALMONT *watches her go, troubled.*)

ELEVEN

Six o'clock in the evening, a couple of days later. The salon in Mme de Tourvel's house, furnished in sombre good taste. MME DE TOURVEL *sits in an armchair, staring blankly at a piece of embroidery. On the other side of the room is an ottoman. Presently,* VALMONT *is shown in by a* FOOTMAN; *as they appear,* MME DE TOURVEL *makes an effort to stand, but is obliged to sit down again almost immediately. She's trembling. The* FOOTMAN *waits for a moment and is surprised to be dismissed impatiently with a gesture from* MME DE TOURVEL. VALMONT, *meanwhile, has bowed deep and now crosses the room to hand* MME DE TOURVEL *a packet of letters, which she takes from him apprehensively. As she inspects them,* VALMONT, *still silent, looks round the room. His eye falls briefly on the ottoman, rests there for a moment and then returns to* MME DE TOURVEL, *who is now looking up at him expectantly.*

VALMONT: I understand Father Anselme has explained to you the reasons for my visit.
TOURVEL: Yes. He said you wished to be reconciled with me before beginning instruction with him.
VALMONT: That's right.
TOURVEL: But I see no need for formal reconciliation, Monsieur.
VALMONT: No? When I have, as you said, insulted you; and when you have treated me with unqualified contempt.
TOURVEL: Contempt? What do you mean?
VALMONT: You run away from my aunt's house in the middle of the night; you refuse to answer or even receive my letters: and all this after I had shown a restraint of which I think we are both aware. I would call that, at the very least, contempt.
TOURVEL: I'm sure you understand me better than you pretend, Monsieur; it seemed to me by far the most . . .
VALMONT: Forgive me, I didn't come here to trade reproaches. You know your virtue has made as deep an impression on

my soul as has your beauty on my heart. I suppose I
imagined that made me worthy of you. What has happened
is probably a just punishment for my presumption.
(*Silence.*)
My life has had no value since you refused to make it
beautiful: all I wanted from this meeting, Madame, was
your forgiveness for the wrongs you think I've done you, so
I can at least end my days in some peace of mind.

TOURVEL: But you won't understand, I couldn't do what you
wanted, my duty wouldn't allow me to . . .
(*Her voice tails off.* VALMONT *moves a little closer and begins
again.*)

VALMONT: It was me you ran away from, wasn't it?

TOURVEL: I had to leave.

VALMONT: And do you have to keep away from me?

TOURVEL: I do.

VALMONT: For ever?

TOURVEL: I must.
(*Silence. Then* VALMONT *changes tack again, moving away
this time.*)

VALMONT: Well. I think you'll find your wish that we be
separated will succeed beyond your wildest dreams.

TOURVEL: Your decision is . . .

VALMONT: It's a function of my despair. I'm as unhappy as you
could ever have wanted me to be.

TOURVEL: I've only ever wanted your happiness.
(VALMONT *moves swiftly to her, falls to his knees and buries
his face in her lap.*)

VALMONT: How can I be happy without you?
(*Cautiously, without answering, as if plunging it into boiling
water,* MME DE TOURVEL *allows her hand to rest for a few
seconds on* VALMONT's *head. Then, as she removes it, he looks
up at her fiercely.*)
I must have you or die.
(MME DE TOURVEL *scrambles to her feet and retreats across
the room.* VALMONT *watches her and then mutters a bitter
aside, loud enough, however, to be heard by her.*)
Death it is.

73

(*Silence.* MME DE TOURVEL *is plainly distraught.* VALMONT *appears to make a great effort to calm himself. He rises to his feet.*)

I'm sorry. I wanted to live for your happiness and I destroyed it. Now I want to give you back your peace of mind and I destroy that too. I'm not used to passion, I can't deal with it. At least, this is the last time. So be calm.

TOURVEL: It's difficult when you are in this state, Monsieur.

VALMONT: Yes; well, don't worry, it won't last very long.

(*He picks up the packet of letters, which* MME DE TOURVEL *has let drop by her chair.*)

These are the only things which might weaken my courage: these deceitful pledges of your friendship. They were all that reconciled me to life.

(*He puts them down on the chair.* MME DE TOURVEL *moves towards him, concerned.*)

TOURVEL: I understood you wanted to return them to me. And that you now approved of the choice my duty has compelled me to make.

VALMONT: Yes. And your choice has determined mine.

TOURVEL: Which is what?

VALMONT: The only choice capable of putting an end to my suffering.

TOURVEL: What do you mean?

(*Her voice is full of fear.* VALMONT *is beside her now and she doesn't resist as he takes her in his arms.*)

VALMONT: Listen. I love you. You've no idea how much. Remember I've made far more difficult sacrifices than the one I'm about to make. Now goodbye.

(*He pulls away from her, but she clutches at his wrist.*)

TOURVEL: No.

VALMONT: Let me go.

TOURVEL: You must listen to me!

VALMONT: I have to go.

TOURVEL: No!

(*She collapses into his arms. He begins to kiss her and she responds: for a moment, they kiss each other greedily. Then he sweeps her up in his arms, carries her across the room, sets her*

74

down gently on the ottoman and kneels alongside her. She bursts into tears and clutches on to him as if she's drowning. He looks down at her as she sobs helplessly and speaks with unusual tenderness.)

VALMONT: Why should you be so upset by the idea of making me happy?

(Gradually, she stops crying and looks up at him.)

TOURVEL: Yes. You're right. I can't live either unless I make you happy. So I promise. No more refusals and no more regrets.

(She kisses him. He begins, slowly, to undress her.)

TWELVE

The following evening. Merteuil's salon. She looks up as VALMONT
bursts ebulliently into the room, outpacing the MAJORDOMO.

VALMONT: Success.
MERTEUIL: At last.
VALMONT: But worth waiting for.
   (MERTEUIL *flashes a chilly look at him, but he's too
   exhilarated to notice.*)
MERTEUIL: So it worked, your foolproof plan?
VALMONT: Of course it wasn't foolproof, I was exaggerating to
   cheer myself up, but I did prepare the ground as carefully
   as I could. And I must say, considering these last few weeks
   my letters were all returned unopened, or rather my letter,
   since I simply placed it every other day in a fresh envelope,
   the result has been a genuine triumph.
   (*By this time, he's taken a seat and he pauses, beaming
   complacently at* MERTEUIL.)
MERTEUIL: And the plan?
VALMONT: I discovered, by intercepting her correspondence in
   the usual way, that she had very wisely decided to change
   her confidante and was pouring out all her inmost thoughts
   to my aunt. So very subtly, and aided by the fact I looked
   terminally exhausted as a result of my exertions with Cécile,
   I began to hint to my aunt that I was losing the will to live,
   knowing that this would be passed on. At the same time, I
   began corresponding with her confessor, an amiably
   dim-witted Cistercian, whom I more or less forced to
   arrange the meeting with her, in return for the privilege of
   being allowed to save my soul, a privilege he will now, poor
   man, be obliged to forgo. So, the threat of suicide, the
   promise of reform.
MERTEUIL: I'm afraid I can't say I find that very original.
VALMONT: Effective though.
MERTEUIL: Tell me about it.

VALMONT: Well, I arrived about six . . .

MERTEUIL: Yes, I think you may omit the details of the seduction, they're never very enlivening: just describe the event itself.

VALMONT: It was . . . unprecedented.

MERTEUIL: Really?

VALMONT: It had a kind of charm I don't think I've ever experienced before. Once she'd surrendered, she behaved with perfect candour. Total mutual delirium: which for the first time ever with me outlasted the pleasure itself. She was astonishing. So much so that I ended by falling on my knees and pledging her eternal love. And do you know, at the time, and for several hours afterwards, I actually meant it!

MERTEUIL: I see.

VALMONT: It's extraordinary, isn't it?

MERTEUIL: Is it? It sounds to me perfectly commonplace.

VALMONT: No, no, I assure you. But of course the best thing about it is that I am now in a position to be able to claim my reward.

(*Silence.* MERTEUIL *considers him coldly for a moment.*)

MERTEUIL: You mean to say you persuaded her to write you a letter as well, in the course of this awesome encounter?

VALMONT: No. I didn't necessarily think you were going to be a stickler for formalities.

MERTEUIL: Do you know, Vicomte, even if you had arrived with a letter up your sleeve, I'm not sure I wouldn't have had to declare our arrangement null and void?

VALMONT: What do you mean?

MERTEUIL: I'm not accustomed to being taken for granted.

VALMONT: But there's no question of that, my dear. You mustn't misunderstand me. What in another case might be taken for presumption, between us, can surely be accepted as a sign of our friendship and confidence in each other. Can't it?

MERTEUIL: I've no wish to tear you away from the arms of someone so astonishing.

VALMONT: We've always been frank with one another.

77

MERTEUIL: And, as a matter of fact, I have also taken a new lover, who, at the moment, is proving more than satisfactory.

VALMONT: Oh? And who is that?

MERTEUIL: I am not in the mood for confidences this evening. Don't let me keep you.
(*Silence. For a moment,* VALMONT *is at a loss. Then he decides to persevere.*)

VALMONT: You can't seriously imagine there's a woman in the world I could ever prefer to you?

MERTEUIL: I'm sure you're quite willing to accept me as an addition to your harem.

VALMONT: No, no, you've misinterpreted. What you think is vanity, taking you for granted: it's really only eagerness.
(MERTEUIL's *expression softens slightly, for the first time.* VALMONT *is quick to sense this and immediately tries to press home his advantage.*)
I'd sacrifice anything or anybody to you, you know that.

MERTEUIL: All right, Vicomte, let's try to discuss this calmly, shall we, like friends?

VALMONT: By all means.

MERTEUIL: There's a strange thing about pleasure, haven't you noticed? It's the only thing that brings the sexes together; and yet it's not sufficient in itself to form the basis of a relationship. You see, unless there's some element of love involved, pleasure must lead directly to disgust.

VALMONT: I'm not sure I agree with that.

MERTEUIL: Now, fortunately, it's only necessary for this love to exist on one side. The partner who feels it is naturally the happier; while the partner who doesn't is to some extent compensated by the pleasures of deceit.

VALMONT: I don't think I see your point.

MERTEUIL: My point, Vicomte, is that you and I can in no way conform to this essential pattern, and we may as well admit it. Cardsharps sit at separate tables.

VALMONT: Yes, and then they compare notes.

MERTEUIL: Maybe: but without, I think, dealing a new hand.

VALMONT: I can't entirely accept the analogy.

MERTEUIL: Don't worry: I shan't go back on our agreement. I
have to go away for a couple of weeks . . .

VALMONT: What for?

MERTEUIL: A private matter.

VALMONT: There was a time you kept no secrets from me.

MERTEUIL: Don't you want me to finish what I was saying?

VALMONT: Of course, I'm sorry.

MERTEUIL: When I've returned, and on receipt of this famous
letter, you and I will spend a single night together. I'm sure
we shall find it quite sufficient. We shall enjoy it enough to
regret that it's to be our last; but then we shall remember
that regret is an essential component of happiness. And part
the best of friends.

VALMONT: I think we should take it one step at a time, don't
you?

MERTEUIL: No. I think we should be under no illusions.

VALMONT: You see, I don't think I've ever been unfaithful to
you.

MERTEUIL: You know, Vicomte, instead of trying to work on
me in this, let's be frank, mechanical fashion, you should
be thanking me.

VALMONT: What for?

MERTEUIL: My courage. My stout resistance. My
clear-sightedness. I understand, you see, what's going on.

VALMONT: Well, that's more than I can claim.

MERTEUIL: I know. You may genuinely be unaware of this. But
I can see quite plainly that you're in love with this woman.

VALMONT: No. You're wrong. Not at all.

MERTEUIL: Have you forgotten what it's like to make a woman
happy; and to be made happy yourself?

VALMONT: I . . . of course not.

MERTEUIL: We loved each other once, didn't we? I think it was
love. And you made me very happy.

VALMONT: And I could again. We just untied the knot, it was
never broken. It was nothing but a temporary . . . failure of
the imagination.

MERTEUIL: No, no. There would have to be sacrifices you
couldn't make and I wouldn't deserve.

VALMONT: But I told you: any sacrifice you ask.

MERTEUIL: Illusions, of course, are by their nature sweet.

VALMONT: I have no illusions. I lost them on my travels. Now I
want to come home. As for this present infatuation, it won't
last. But, for the moment, it's beyond my control.

(*Silence. She looks at him for a moment, considering.*)

MERTEUIL: You'll be the first to know when I return.

VALMONT: Make it soon. I want it to be very soon.

(*He kisses her. She seems on the point of submitting to a long
kiss, but then she breaks away abruptly and speaks with her
usual control.*)

MERTEUIL: Goodbye.

(VALMONT *bows and hurries from the room.* MERTEUIL
*stands a moment, collecting herself, then she crosses the room
and opens a door.*)

He's gone.

(*Presently,* DANCENY *steps into the room. He embraces her
impulsively and, once again, she submits only briefly.*)

DANCENY: I thought he'd be here all night. Time has no logic
when I'm not with you: an hour is like a century.

MERTEUIL: We shall get on a good deal better if you make a
concerted effort not to sound like the latest novel.

(DANCENY *blushes.*)

DANCENY: I'm sorry, I . . .

(MERTEUIL *softens and reaches a hand to his cheek.*)

MERTEUIL: Never mind. Take me upstairs.

(*Arm in arm, they begin to move towards the door.*)

THIRTEEN

A fortnight later. Afternoon. The salon in Valmont's house.
VALMONT *is pouring another glass of champagne for* ÉMILIE, *when his* FOOTMAN *enters the room and murmurs something in his ear, which evidently gives him an unpleasant surprise. He controls himself quickly however, gives some instructions and, as the* FOOTMAN *hurries out, turns to* ÉMILIE.

VALMONT: Drink up.
ÉMILIE: What is it?
VALMONT: Someone who might well not appreciate your presence here.
ÉMILIE: You mean a woman.
VALMONT: A lady, we might even say.
ÉMILIE: Oh, well, then.
　　(She tosses back her champagne and rises to her feet; then, a thought strikes her.)
Not the one you wrote that letter to?
VALMONT: The very one.
ÉMILIE: I enjoyed that.
VALMONT: And you proved a most talented desk.
ÉMILIE: I'd love to see what she looks like.
VALMONT: Well, you can't.
　　(He moves over to her as she makes a face of mock disappointment, ready to hustle her out of the room. As he reaches her, however, he seems to hesitate a moment, considering.)
On second thoughts, I don't see why you shouldn't.
ÉMILIE: Oo.
VALMONT: As long as there's no bad behaviour.
ÉMILIE: Never unless required.
　　(VALMONT looks at her thoughtfully.)
VALMONT: Where's your Dutchman?
ÉMILIE: Safe in Holland, far as I know.
VALMONT: And do you have an appointment for tonight?

ÉMILIE: Few friends for dinner.

VALMONT: And after dinner?

ÉMILIE: Nothing firm.

(VALMONT *crosses to his desk, opens a drawer and takes out, as before, a small bag of money.*)

VALMONT: Then perhaps I shall call round on you later.

(*He moves over to her and hands her the money, just as the* FOOTMAN *is showing in* MME DE TOURVEL, *who stops on the threshold, startled by what she sees.*)

ÉMILIE: I'll be there.

(*She leaves the room, staring with undisguised fascination at* MME DE TOURVEL, *who looks back at her, miserably confused.* VALMONT *is hovering, torn between his desire to greet* MME DE TOURVEL *and his curiosity to see what will happen. It seems as if nothing will; but at the last minute, as she's passing* MME DE TOURVEL, ÉMILIE *is suddenly convulsed with mirth and leaves the room helplessly shaking with laughter.* MME DE TOURVEL *watches her, horrified; and* VALMONT, *concerned now, hurries over to her.*)

VALMONT: This is an unexpected pleasure.

TOURVEL: Evidently.

VALMONT: Take no notice of Émilie; she's notoriously eccentric.

TOURVEL: I know that woman.

VALMONT: Are you sure? I'd be surprised.

TOURVEL: She's been pointed out to me at the Opéra.

VALMONT: Ah, well, yes, she is striking.

TOURVEL: She's a courtesan.

(*Silence.*)

Isn't she?

VALMONT: I suppose in a manner of speaking . . .

(*But* MME DE TOURVEL *suddenly turns away, her eyes full of tears, and makes to hurry out of the room.* VALMONT *catches her arm.*)

TOURVEL: Let me go.

VALMONT: But what's got into you?

TOURVEL: I'm sorry I've disturbed you.

VALMONT: Of course you haven't disturbed me, I'm overjoyed to see you.

TOURVEL: Please let me go now.

VALMONT: No, no, I can't, this is absurd.

TOURVEL: Let go!

(*She wrenches free and he has to cut her off bodily as she makes a determined effort to leave. By now, she's sobbing blindly.*)

VALMONT: No, wait, wait a minute, it never occurred to me you'd assume, you must let me explain . . .

TOURVEL: No!

VALMONT: Let's sit down calmly . . .

TOURVEL: And you will never be received at my house again!

VALMONT: Now.

(*He's pinioning her in his arms. She struggles violently for a moment and then goes limp. He helps her across to a sofa and sits them both down, keeping an arm round her.*)

Now listen.

TOURVEL: I don't want your lies and excuses!

VALMONT: Just listen to me. Just hear me out, that's all I ask, then you can judge.

TOURVEL: I don't want to.

VALMONT: Have a glass of champagne . . .

TOURVEL: No!

(*But for some reason, though still trembling, she quietens down and watches him, transfixed, as he speaks with unruffled calm.*)

VALMONT: Unfortunately, I cannot unlive the years I lived before I met you; and, as I've explained to you before, during those years, I had a wide acquaintance, the majority of whom were no doubt undesirable in one respect or another. Now it may surprise you to know that Émilie, in common with many others of her profession and character, is kind-hearted enough to take an interest in those less fortunate than herself. She has, in short, the free time and the inclination to do a great deal of charity work: donations to hospitals, soup for the poor, protection for animals, anything which touches her sentimental heart. From time to time, I make small contributions to her purse. That's all.

TOURVEL: Is that true?

VALMONT: My relations with Émilie have for some years now

been quite blameless. She's even done a little secretarial work for me on occasion. Since I now know your feelings on the matter, I shall of course take steps to make sure she is never received here again.

TOURVEL: Why did she laugh?

VALMONT: I've no idea. Malice perhaps? Jealousy? Girls of that class are often unpredictable. I'm at a loss to explain it.

TOURVEL: Well, does she know about me?

VALMONT: No doubt she made what, in view of my past, must be accepted as a fair assumption.

(*Silence.* MME DE TOURVEL *looks at him, almost convinced.*)

TOURVEL: I want to believe you.

VALMONT: I knew you were coming up, you were announced. Do you seriously imagine, if I'd felt the slightest guilt about Émilie, I would have allowed you to see her here?

TOURVEL: I suppose not.

VALMONT: No.

TOURVEL: I'm sorry.

VALMONT: No, no, no, it's I who must apologize. It was most insensitive of me. Some relics of my old persona remain. That was the thoughtless action of a man who had never met you.

(MME DE TOURVEL *begins to weep again, but softly this time, relieved. She buries her face in* VALMONT's *chest. He watches her for a moment, his expression profoundly contented.*)

I didn't think it was possible for me to love you more, but your jealousy . . .

(*He breaks off; and now he too seems genuinely moved. Presently,* MME DE TOURVEL *looks up at him.*)

TOURVEL: I love you so much.

(*He continues to look at her, disarmed by her sincerity, suddenly no longer in command of his emotions, his expression pained and uncharacteristically tender.*)

FOURTEEN

Ten days later. Evening. Mme de Merteuil's salon. A domestic tableau. DANCENY *lies on the sofa with his head in* MERTEUIL's *lap. She plays idly with his hair. After a time, at first unseen by the others and unaccompanied by servants,* VALMONT *appears in the doorway. He assesses the scene and then clears his throat, causing* DANCENY *to shoot upwards in confusion.* MERTEUIL *looks at* VALMONT, *her eyes cold.*

VALMONT: Your porter appears to be under the impression that you are still out of town.

MERTEUIL: I have in fact only just returned.

VALMONT: Without attracting the attention of your porter? I think it may be time to review your domestic arrangements.

MERTEUIL: I'm exhausted from the journey. Naturally I instructed my porter to inform casual callers that I was out. (VALMONT *seems to check a retort at this point, and turns instead, smiling, to* DANCENY.)

VALMONT: And you here, as well, my dear young friend. The porter would appear to be having a somewhat erratic evening.

DANCENY: Oh, well, I, erm, yes.

VALMONT: I'm glad to find you, I've been trying to contact you for some days.

DANCENY: Have you?

VALMONT: Mademoiselle Cécile returns to Paris after an absence of over two months. What do you suppose is uppermost in her mind? Answer, of course, the longed-for reunion with her beloved Chevalier.

MERTEUIL: Vicomte, this is no time to make mischief.

VALMONT: Nothing could be further from my mind, Madame.

DANCENY: Go on.

VALMONT: Imagine her distress and alarm when her loved one is apparently nowhere to be found. I've had to do more improvising than an Italian actor.

DANCENY: But how is she? Is she all right?

VALMONT: Oh, yes. Well, no, to be quite frank with you. I'm sorry to tell you she's been ill.

(DANCENY *springs to his feet, horrified.*)

DANCENY: Ill!

VALMONT: Whether it was brought on by her anxieties it's impossible to say, but it seems about a week ago they were compelled to send for the surgeon in the middle of the night, and for a while he was very concerned.

DANCENY: But this is terrible!

VALMONT: Calm yourself, my friend, she has been declared well on the road to recovery and she is convalescing now. But you can well imagine how desperate I've been to find you.

DANCENY: Of course, my God, how could I have not been here at such a time? How can I ever forgive myself?

(VALMONT *chooses not to answer this: he looks at* MERTEUIL *for a moment, assessing the damage.*)

VALMONT: But look, I hate to be the bearer of bad tidings. All is well now with Cécile, I assure you, I have it from the surgeon himself. And I shan't disturb you further.

(*He produces a piece of paper from an inside pocket.*)

It's just that I had a letter, the contents of which I thought might be of interest to the Marquise.

(*Silence. The ball is in* MERTEUIL's *court and she makes the effort to reach a decision.*)

MERTEUIL: I think perhaps I should spend a few minutes with the Vicomte on a private matter. Why don't you go upstairs, I shan't be long.

DANCENY: But I'm worried about Cécile.

MERTEUIL: I don't think there's anything to be done at this hour of the evening. You can send to enquire after her tomorrow.

DANCENY: Well, all right, if you say so.

MERTEUIL: I do.

DANCENY: I'm sorry, Vicomte, I . . .

VALMONT: Don't upset yourself, dear boy, everything is as it should be.

DANCENY: Thank you. Thank you.

(*He leaves the room. Silence.* MERTEUIL *is about to speak,*
when VALMONT *interrupts her by handing her the letter.*
MERTEUIL *gives it a cursory glance and then hands it back to*
VALMONT.)

MERTEUIL: I see she writes as badly as she dresses.

VALMONT: I think I'm right in saying that in this case it's the
content not the style which is the essential. But perhaps
there's something else we should discuss first.

MERTEUIL: I do hope you're not going to be difficult about
Danceny: it was a complete coincidence he arrived at the
gates at the same moment as my carriage.

VALMONT: Really, my love, this is hardly worthy of you. Given
the uncharacteristic mystery you made about the identity of
your new lover and Danceny's and your simultaneous
disappearance from Paris, I would have to have been a good
deal stupider even than you seem to assume I am, not to
have reached the obvious conclusion. If Danceny and your
carriage arrived at the gates at the same moment, I imagine
the main reason was because he was in it.

MERTEUIL: You're quite right, of course.

VALMONT: And furthermore, I happen to know that this
moment of which we speak occurred two days ago.

MERTEUIL: Your spies are efficient.

VALMONT: So much for my being the first to know when you
returned. A lesser man might allow himself to get angry.

MERTEUIL: Such a man might risk losing his ability to charm,
without necessarily enhancing his power to persuade.
(*Silence.* VALMONT *restrains himself and decides to change*
tack.)

VALMONT: I must say I'm not surprised you chose to be reticent
about so manifestly unsuitable a lover.

MERTEUIL: My motive had nothing whatever to do with his
suitability.

VALMONT: I mean I know Belleroche was pretty limp, but I
think you could have found a livelier replacement than that
mawkish schoolboy.

MERTEUIL: Mawkish or not, he's completely devoted to me,
and, I suspect, better equipped to provide me with

happiness and pleasure than you in your present mood.

VALMONT: I see.

(*Slightly winded by this, he lapses into an injured silence.*
MERTEUIL's *mood, however, now she has regained the
initiative, seems to have improved.*)

MERTEUIL: So is it really true the little one has been ill?

VALMONT: Not so much an illness, more a refurbishment.

MERTEUIL: What can you mean?

(VALMONT's *energy returns at the prospect of telling his story.*)

VALMONT: Once she'd returned to Paris, some money for the
porter and a few flowers for his wife were enough to enable
me to resume my nocturnal visits: which, incidentally,
don't you agree, shows up Danceny's initiative in a very
poor light. However, the ease of it no doubt made us over-
confident, and one night last week, as we were resting after
our exertions, the door, which we'd forgotten to lock,
suddenly blew open. The most dreadful shock. Cécile threw
herself out of bed and tried to jam herself between it and
the wall. A sudden severe backache gave way to some
unmistakable symptoms. After that, it was a real test of
ingenuity, getting the surgeon round, without giving
ourselves away.

MERTEUIL: But you evidently succeeded?

VALMONT: Can you imagine, my dear, it turned out Cécile
wasn't even aware of being pregnant in the first place. She
certainly doesn't devote any undue energy to thinking.

MERTEUIL: Well, Vicomte, I'm sorry about the loss of your son
and Gercourt's heir.

VALMONT: Oh, I thought you'd be pleased, you seemed notably
disgruntled about it when I first told you.

MERTEUIL: Once I got used to the idea, I began to enjoy it. I
think you should make another attempt, don't you?

VALMONT: I rather felt the moment had come to pass her on to
young Danceny.

(*Silence.* MERTEUIL *considers for a moment.*)

MERTEUIL: No, I'm not sure that would be advisable just now.

VALMONT: Oh, you don't?

(*Silence.*)

MERTEUIL: If I thought you would be your old charming self, I might invite you to visit me one evening next week.

VALMONT: Really.

MERTEUIL: I still love you, you see, in spite of all your faults and my complaints.

VALMONT: I'm touched. What else will you exact before honouring your obligations?

(*There's a pause, during which* MERTEUIL *looks mischievously at* VALMONT.)

MERTEUIL: I have a friend, who became involved, as sometimes happens, with an entirely unsuitable woman. Whenever any of us pointed this out to him, he invariably made the same feeble reply: it's beyond my control, he would say. He was on the verge of becoming a laughing-stock. At which point, another friend of mine, a woman, decided to speak to him seriously, and, most importantly, drew his attention to this linguistic foible, of which he'd previously been unaware, and told him his name was in danger of becoming ludicrously associated with this phrase for the rest of his life. So do you know what he did?

VALMONT: I feel sure you're about to tell me.

MERTEUIL: He went round to see his mistress and bluntly announced he was leaving her. As you might expect, she protested vociferously. But to everything she said, to every objection she made, he simply replied: it's beyond my control.

(*Long silence. Eventually,* VALMONT *rises.*)

VALMONT: I must leave you to your lessons.

(MERTEUIL *doesn't answer. She watches him, smiling, as he moves, deep in thought, towards the door.*)

FIFTEEN

The following afternoon. The salon in Mme de Tourvel's house. As her FOOTMAN *shows in* VALMONT, *she springs to her feet, unable to conceal her delight. He however looks strained and weary and advances almost reluctantly into the room, as the* FOOTMAN *leaves them.* MME DE TOURVEL *runs over to him and buries herself in his arms. He embraces her almost involuntarily, bracing himself against what is to come.*

TOURVEL: You're only five minutes late, but I get so frightened. I become convinced I'm never going to see you again.
(VALMONT *carefully disentangles himself and puts some distance between them before he speaks.*)

VALMONT: My angel.

TOURVEL: Is it like that for you?

VALMONT: Oh, yes. At the moment, for example, I'm quite convinced I'm never going to see you again.
(*Silence.* TOURVEL *frowns, trying to make sense of this.*)

TOURVEL: What?

VALMONT: I'm so bored, you see. It's beyond my control.

TOURVEL: What do you mean?

VALMONT: After all, it's been four months. So, what I say. It's beyond my control.

TOURVEL: Do you mean . . . do you mean you don't love me any more?

VALMONT: My love had great difficulty outlasting your virtue. It's beyond my control.

TOURVEL: It's that woman, isn't it?

VALMONT: You're quite right, I have been deceiving you with Émilie. Among others. It's beyond my control.

TOURVEL: Why are you doing this?

VALMONT: Perhaps your merciless vulnerability has driven me to it. Anyway, it's beyond my control.

TOURVEL: I can't believe this is happening.

VALMONT: There's a woman. Not Émilie, another woman. A

woman I adore. And I'm afraid she's insisting I give you up. It's beyond my control.

(*Suddenly,* MME DE TOURVEL *rushes at him, fists flailing. They grapple silently and grimly for a moment, before she screams at him.*)

TOURVEL: Liar!

VALMONT: You're right, I am a liar. It's like your fidelity, a fact of life, no more nor less irritating. Certainly, it's beyond my control.

TOURVEL: Stop it, don't keep saying that!

VALMONT: Sorry. It's beyond my control.

(MME DE TOURVEL *screams.*)

Why don't you take another lover?

(*She bursts into tears, shaking her head and moaning incoherently.*)

Just as you like, of course. It's beyond my control.

TOURVEL: Do you want to kill me?

(VALMONT *strides over to her, takes her by the hair and jerks her head up, shocking her into a moment's silence.*)

VALMONT: Listen. Listen to me. You've given me great pleasure. But I just can't bring myself to regret leaving you. It's the way of the world. Quite beyond my control.

(*When he lets go of her hair, she collapses full-length, moaning and sobbing helplessly.* VALMONT *crosses to the doorway and turns to look back at her. His triumphant expression has lasted only a moment; and now gives way to a queasy, haunted, tormented look. His eyes are full of fear and regret. For a moment, it's almost as if he's going to run back to help her; but, abruptly, he turns and guiltily scuttles away.*)

SIXTEEN

*About a week later. A December evening in Mme de Merteuil's
salon.* MERTEUIL *sits at a small escritoire, writing. After a time,*
VALMONT *appears in the doorway, once again unannounced.*
MERTEUIL, *with her back to the door, doesn't see him, but as he
approaches, she looks up, hearing a footstep, and speaks without
turning round.*

MERTEUIL: Is that you? You're early.

VALMONT: Am I?

> (MERTEUIL *spins around, startled; to be greeted with an ironic
> bow from* VALMONT.)

I wanted to ask you: that story you told me, how did it end?

MERTEUIL: I'm not sure I know what you mean.

VALMONT: Well, once this friend of yours had taken the advice
of his lady-friend, did she take him back?

MERTEUIL: Am I to understand . . . ?

VALMONT: The day after our last meeting, I broke with
Madame de Tourvel. On the grounds that it was beyond my
control.

> (*A slow smile of great satisfaction spreads across* MERTEUIL's
> *face.*)

MERTEUIL: You didn't!

VALMONT: I certainly did.

MERTEUIL: Seriously?

VALMONT: On my honour.

MERTEUIL: But how wonderful of you. I never thought you'd
do it.

VALMONT: It seemed pointless to delay.

MERTEUIL: With the anticipated results?

VALMONT: She was prostrate when I left. I called back the
following day.

MERTEUIL: You went back?

VALMONT: Yes, but she declined to receive me.

MERTEUIL: You don't say.

VALMONT: Subsequent enquiries I made established that she
    had withdrawn to a convent.

MERTEUIL: Indeed.

VALMONT: And she's still there. A very fitting conclusion,
    really. It's as if she'd been widowed.

    (*He reflects for a moment, then turns to her, radiating*
    confidence.)

    You kept telling me my reputation was in danger, but I
    think this may well turn out to be my most famous exploit.
    I believe it sets a new standard. I think I could confidently
    offer it as a challenge to any potential rival for my position.
    Only one thing could possibly bring me greater glory.

MERTEUIL: What's that?

VALMONT: To win her back.

MERTEUIL: You think you could?

VALMONT: I don't see why not.

MERTEUIL: I'll tell you why not: because when one woman
    strikes at the heart of another, she seldom misses; and the
    wound is invariably fatal.

VALMONT: Is that so?

MERTEUIL: I'm so convinced it's so, I'm prepared to offer any
    odds you care to suggest against your success.

    (*Some of the self-satisfaction has ebbed out of* VALMONT's
    expression.)

    You see, I'm also inclined to see this as one of my greatest
    triumphs.

VALMONT: There's nothing a woman enjoys as much as a
    victory over another woman.

MERTEUIL: Except, you see, Vicomte, my victory wasn't over
    her.

VALMONT: Of course it was, what do you mean?

MERTEUIL: It was over you.

    (*Long silence. The fear returns to* VALMONT's *eyes. He begins*
    to look concerned. MERTEUIL, *on the other hand, has never*
    seemed more serene.)

    That's what's so amusing. That's what's so genuinely
    delicious.

VALMONT: You don't know what you're talking about.

MERTEUIL: You loved that woman, Vicomte. What's more you still do. Quite desperately. If you hadn't been so ashamed of it, how could you possibly have treated her so viciously? You couldn't bear even the vague possibility of being laughed at. And this has proved something I've always suspected. That vanity and happiness are incompatible.

(VALMONT *is very shaken. He's forced to make a great effort, before he can resume, his voice a touch ragged with strain.*)

VALMONT: Whatever may or may not be the truth of these philosophical speculations, the fact is it's now your turn to make a sacrifice.

MERTEUIL: Is that right?

VALMONT: Danceny must go.

MERTEUIL: Where?

VALMONT: I've been more than patient about this little whim of yours, but enough is enough and I really must insist you call a halt to it.

(*Silence.*)

MERTEUIL: One of the reasons I never remarried, despite a quite bewildering range of offers, was the determination never again to be ordered around. I decided if I felt like telling a lie, I'd rather do it for fun than because I had no alternative. So I must ask you to adopt a less marital tone of voice.

VALMONT: She's ill, you know. I've made her ill. For your sake. So the least you can do is get rid of that colourless youth.

MERTEUIL: I should have thought you'd have had enough of bullying women for the time being.

(VALMONT's *face hardens.*)

VALMONT: Right. I see I shall have to make myself very plain. I've come to spend the night. I shall not take at all kindly to being turned away.

(MERTEUIL *briefly consults the clock on her desk.*)

MERTEUIL: I am sorry. I'm afraid I've made other arrangements.

(*A grim satisfaction begins to enliven* VALMONT's *features.*)

VALMONT: Ah. I knew there was something. Something I had to tell you. What with one thing and another, it had slipped my mind.

MERTEUIL: What?

VALMONT: Danceny isn't coming. Not tonight.

MERTEUIL: What do you mean? How do you know?

VALMONT: I know because I've arranged for him to spend the
night with Cécile.

(*He smiles charmingly at her.*)

Now I come to think of it, he did mention he was expected
here. But when I put it to him that he really would have to
make a choice, I must say he didn't hesitate for a second.
I'd dictated a letter for Cécile to send him, as insurance, but
as it turned out, there wasn't any need to be so cautious. He
knew his mind.

MERTEUIL: And now I know yours.

VALMONT: He's coming to see you tomorrow to explain and to
offer you, do I have this right, yes, I think so, his eternal
friendship. As you said, he's completely devoted to you.

MERTEUIL: That's enough, Vicomte.

VALMONT: You're absolutely right. Shall we go up?

MERTEUIL: Shall we what?

VALMONT: Go up. Unless you prefer, this, if memory serves,
rather purgatorial sofa.

MERTEUIL: I believe it's time you were going.

(*Silence.*)

VALMONT: No. I don't think so. We made an arrangement. I
really don't think I can allow myself to be taken advantage
of a moment longer.

MERTEUIL: Remember I'm better at this than you are.

VALMONT: Perhaps. But it's always the best swimmers who
drown. Now. Yes or no? Up to you, of course. I wouldn't
dream of trying to influence you. I therefore confine myself
to remarking that a no will be regarded as a declaration of
war. So. One single word is all that's required.

MERTEUIL: All right.

(*She looks at him evenly for a moment, almost long enough for
him to conclude that she has made her answer. But she hasn't.
It follows now, calm and authoritative.*)

War.

(*Blackout.*)

95

Dawn on a misty December morning in the Bois de Vincennes. On one side of the stage, VALMONT *and* AZOLAN: *on the other,* DANCENY *and a* MANSERVANT. VALMONT *is making his selection from a case of épées, held open for him by* AZOLAN. *He weighs now one and now the other in his hand.* DANCENY, *meanwhile, waits impatiently, in shirt-sleeves, épée in hand, shifting from one foot to the other. Finally, as* VALMONT *seems to be on the point of making his decision,* DANCENY *can restrain himself no further.*

DANCENY: I know it was easy for you to make a fool of me when I trusted you, but out here I think you'll find there's very little room for trickery!
(*His* MANSERVANT *looks at him disapprovingly, but* VALMONT *responds calmly to this breach of etiquette.*)
VALMONT: I recommend you conserve your energy for the business in hand.
(*He makes his final choice of épée and lays it on the ground while* AZOLAN *helps him off with his coat and on with a black glove. Then,* VALMONT *and* DANCENY *approach one another and take up the en-garde position. At a sign from* AZOLAN, *the duel begins, fierce and determined,* VALMONT's *skill against* DANCENY's *aggression. For some time, they're evenly matched, with* VALMONT, *if anything, looking the more dangerous. Then* DANCENY *succeeds, more by luck than good judgement, in wounding* VALMONT *in whichever is not his sword arm. A short pause ensues and then, after a murmured consultation between* VALMONT *and* AZOLAN, *the duellists resume the en-garde position and begin again. This time it's* DANCENY *who looks to have the initiative. For some reason, connected or not with his wound,* VALMONT *seems to have lost heart, or even interest, and at one point when the deflection of a too-committed attack by* DANCENY *seems to leave him wide open,* VALMONT *fails to take advantage of what looks like a golden opportunity. Eventually, it's some piece of inattention very close to*

96

carelessness on VALMONT's *part which allows* DANCENY *through his guard with a thrust which enters* VALMONT's *body somewhere just below his heart. There's a moment of mutual shock, and then* DANCENY *withdraws his sword and* VALMONT *staggers a couple of steps towards him, before subsiding with a slight gasp to the ground.* AZOLAN *hurries to him, falls to one knee and lifts* VALMONT's *head.*)

I'm cold.

(AZOLAN *runs to get* VALMONT's *coat, as* DANCENY *turns to his* MANSERVANT.)

DANCENY: Fetch the surgeon.

VALMONT: No, no.

DANCENY: Do as I say.

(*The* MANSERVANT *hurries away as* AZOLAN *manages to drape* VALMONT's *coat around him.* DANCENY *stands alone, uneasy, some way off, so that* VALMONT *has to make the considerable effort to raise his voice above a murmur, to be sure that* DANCENY *will hear him.*)

VALMONT: A moment of your time.

(DANCENY *reluctantly approaches.* VALMONT *begins to try to struggle up on one elbow, and* AZOLAN *drops to one knee to support him.*)

Two things: a word of advice, which of course you may ignore, but it is honestly intended; and a request.

(*He pauses, a little breathless.*)

DANCENY: Go on.

VALMONT: The advice is: be careful of the Marquise de Merteuil.

DANCENY: You must permit me to treat with scepticism anything you have to say about her.

VALMONT: Nevertheless, I must tell you: in this affair, both of us are her creatures.

(DANCENY *looks at him thoughtfully, not answering for a moment.*)

DANCENY: And the request?

VALMONT: I want you to get somehow to see Madame de Tourvel . . .

DANCENY: I understand she's very ill.

VALMONT: That's why this is most important to me. I want you to tell her I can't explain why I broke with her as I did, but that since then, my life has been worth nothing. I pushed the blade in deeper than you just have, my boy, and I want you to help me withdraw it. Tell her it's lucky for her that I've gone and I'm glad not to have to live without her. Tell her her love was the only real happiness I've ever known.

DANCENY: I will.

VALMONT: Thank you.

(*The silence is broken by snatches of birdsong.* DANCENY, *suddenly overcome, puts a hand up to brush away a tear.* AZOLAN, *watching, lets his indignation show.*)

AZOLAN: It's all very well doing that now.

VALMONT: Let him be. He had good cause. It's something I don't believe anyone's ever been able to say about me.

(*He raises a hand towards* DANCENY: *but the effort of doing so is too great, and he slumps back before* DANCENY *can take his hand. He's dead.*)

EIGHTEEN

New Year's Eve. Once again, three ladies at cards in the salon of Mme de Merteuil's hôtel. This time, it's MERTEUIL *herself,* MME DE VOLANGES *and* MME DE ROSEMONDE, *the latter in mourning. For a while, the play proceeds in silence, until it comes to* MME DE ROSEMONDE's *turn and she is looking away, lost in thought, no longer concentrating on the game.* MERTEUIL *discreetly clears her throat, to no effect. Finally* MME DE VOLANGES *leans forward and touches* MME DE ROSEMONDE's *elbow.*

VOLANGES: Madame.

(MME DE ROSEMONDE *comes to with a start.*)

ROSEMONDE: Forgive me. At my age, it seems reasonable to hope to be spared any further personal tragedies. But two in the space of a few days . . .

MERTEUIL: Of course, Madame.

VOLANGES: And I was just thinking: when you were last in Paris, a year ago, do you remember that conversation we had? We were trying to decide who was the happiest and most enviable person we knew; and we both agreed it was Madame de Tourvel.

MERTEUIL: You were with her, were you not, when she died?

VOLANGES: I was with her from the day after she ran away to the convent. I shall never forget those terrible sights. When she kept ripping away the bandages after they bled her. The delirium and the convulsions. How she wasted away.

(MERTEUIL *listens, her practised expressionlessness intact, except for the glitter of satisfaction in her eyes.* MME DE VOLANGES *shakes her head, sighs, resumes.*)

All the same, I think she might have recovered if that unfortunate young man hadn't somehow managed to let her know the Vicomte your nephew was dead. After that, she simply lost the will to live. Apparently, as he was dying, the Vicomte managed to convince Danceny that Madame de Tourvel was the only woman he'd ever loved.

MERTEUIL: That's enough!

(*All of them, even* MERTEUIL *herself, are startled by the sharpness of this involuntary remark.* MERTEUIL *hastens to paper over the crack, by adding a quiet explanation to* MME DE VOLANGES.)

I think we should respect the sensibilities of our friend.

ROSEMONDE: Oh, no, I firmly believe that was the truth.

MERTEUIL: Well, perhaps, I can't see how we shall ever know . . .

(*Her voice is uncharacteristically shaky. She makes an effort to regain her usual self-control and changes the subject.*)

And what news of your daughter?

VOLANGES: She seems quite adamant. I've appealed to her and pleaded with her but she won't budge. I did want to ask your advice about this, both of you. Monsieur de Gercourt is expected back any day now. Is there nothing to be done? Must I really break off such an advantageous match?

MERTEUIL: Oh, surely not.

ROSEMONDE: I'm afraid you must.

VOLANGES: But why?

ROSEMONDE: I'd rather you didn't ask.

MERTEUIL: I think you must provide a reason, Madame, if you ask our friend to sacrifice so glorious a future.

(*Her fighting spirit has returned now, and her voice is as crisp and decisive as ever.*)

VOLANGES: To be honest with you, Madame, and in spite of his crime, I'd rather marry Cécile to Danceny than see my only child become a nun.

ROSEMONDE: As a matter of fact, I've heard from Danceny. He sent me a very strange letter. From Malta.

VOLANGES: Oh, that's where he's run away to?

(*A silence falls.* MERTEUIL *is busy digesting what* MME DE ROSEMONDE *has said. When she's done so, she turns to* MME DE VOLANGES.)

MERTEUIL: On second thoughts, my dear, I suppose it might be best to defer to Madame's wisdom and experience. Perhaps you should leave Cécile in the convent.

VOLANGES: But there must be a reason?

(Silence. No one seems disposed to add anything and MME DE
VOLANGES's *question hangs in the air. Eventually,*
MERTEUIL *speaks, with all her customary authority.)*

MERTEUIL: This has been a terrible few weeks. But time passes
so quickly. A new year tomorrow and more than half-way
through the eighties already. I used to be afraid of growing
old, but now I trust in God and accept. I dare say we would
not be wrong to look forward to whatever the nineties may
bring. Meanwhile, I suggest our best course is to continue
with the game.

*(Her words seem to exert a calming effect on her companions:
and indeed, they resume playing. The atmosphere is serene. Very
slowly, the lights fade; but just before they vanish, there appears
on the back wall, fleeting but sharp, the unmistakable silhouette
of the guillotine.)*